About this Book

In the arc of every leader's life we take furtive glances over our shoulder to assess the status of our followers. Averting one's eyes from what lies ahead is risky with so much coming at you. It's especially disconcerting when you can see your mates falling behind and splitting into dissident groups. Why does this happen and what can be done about it?

For too many, this "disengagement" as Gallup puts it, stems from a lack of trust in the leader's character. Regardless of their other qualities, no thinking person is going to follow a so-called leader into uncertainty without absolute trust in their integrity, moral clarity and courage. Do they have an unwavering moral compass? What's their "fudge factor?" Do they have my best interests at heart? What are they hiding? How do they behave when things get tough?

The purpose of this book is to enable you to answer these questions in such a compelling way that the power and reach of your influence continues to increase over your lifetime. And that path is illuminated by showing how history's greatest leaders, like Lincoln, Mandela and Martin Luther King Jr., achieved "almost omnipotent" influence. More specifically, this book describes how they aligned and integrated their moral, rational and emotional dimensions to create compelling inside-out influence, exceptional critical thinking and decision-making skills, and strong emotional intelligence and resilience.

Absent this healthy psychological alignment and integration we experience inner conflict, stress and cognitive dysfunction spilling over into all our relationships and leadership efforts.

This book defines what moral leadership is, why it is critical to our happiness and success, how others are influenced by it, and how to summit the peaks of moral clarity and courage to dramatically increase your leadership effectiveness.

The Power of Moral Leadership addresses these fundamental questions with compelling answers based on extensive research, examples of how great leaders developed moral clarity and courage, how they used it to achieve exceptional results, and more practical lessons from the author's personal leadership journey at FedEx and in his leadership development practice.

More Praise for
The Power of Moral Leadership

"This is way beyond another business book. It is also about choices we make and how those impact ourselves and others. Roy has translated his experience, education, and wisdom into principles that are easy to understand and apply. His excellent deep dives into the Golden Rule, the current state of moral leadership, and its impact on culture and performance go well beyond where many of us stopped processing. Roy's book has already had a positive impact on my life and I firmly believe team members at every level will benefit by reading it."

—Steve Nielsen, former Managing Director, FedEx Leadership Institute & Senior Consultant, Center for Management & Organization Effectiveness.

"Put simply, I would strongly recommend *The Power of Moral Leadership* to all leaders who want to improve. Indeed, in a world where trust in leaders and organisations is perceived to be in crisis, where leaders perceive that their challenges are growing in number and complexity, it is an absolute must read. Roy argues with passion for the need for leaders to be drawn back to timeless and universal principles and behaviours that will enhance their decision-making and integrity. Such principles can provide a powerful compass for leaders to call on to improve their cultures, improve engagement with stakeholders, and improve performance. He successfully argues his point, aided by weaving relevant and wonderful stories throughout, including his own. I challenge anyone to read *The Power of Moral Leadership* and not come away reflecting on the moral implications of every thought, decision and action they have made."

—David Ross, Founder and Managing Director, Phoenix Strategic Management and author of *Confronting The Storm*

"Roy's passion to continuously learn and advance the theory and practice of leadership is unparalleled. *The Power of Moral Leadership* is packed with real-world case studies, lessons learned and practical suggestions for improving our leadership in a way that directly improves the bottom line. He frames the whole idea of "Leadership" as the ability to positively influence others, gain their respect and trust, and to consequently achieve results that bring value to everybody involved. Looking at it from such perspective makes it simple to understand why being a better leader should be everybody's mission in business, as in life. This book will jumpstart that journey."

—Marco Busi, Managing Partner, AIKON Ventures; Interim Executive (CEO/COO); Editor-in-Chief, Emerald Publishing; author of *Doing Research That Matters: Shaping the Future of Management*

THE POWER OF
MORAL
LEADERSHIP

THE POWER OF
MORAL
LEADERSHIP

A Timeless Guide to Increasing your Influence,
Emotional Intelligence and Inner Peace

ROY HOLLEY
Foreword by Bill Catlette

ISBN: 979-8-9873628-0-8 (paperback)
ISBN: 979-8-9873628-1-5 (ebook)
ISBN: 979-8-9873628-2-2 (hardcover)

Cover and Interior Design: Creative Publishing Book Design

Printed in the United States of America and Canada

For Xia Guizhen, Melissa, Eric & Alan

Contents

Foreword

The Power of Moral Leadership is a weighty and rather lofty title for a book, especially a business book. Much more than an academic exercise, the book's brand promise is that leaders who follow the precepts contained within will achieve substantially higher levels of employee engagement and followership, corollary discretionary effort, speed of execution, and in turn, operating performance with direct linkage to the bottom line. Moreover, the involved leaders will earn reputations as talent magnets, and will actually like themselves better. You read that correctly.

Roy Holley didn't come upon this "Moral Leadership" idea in a book or a think tank. He experienced it firsthand and had nearly daily reinforcement while working for a young startup high-priority logistics business founded by a combat-hardened and decorated US Marine who also happened to have a diploma from Yale, Frederick W. Smith. The organization was FedEx, nee Federal Express.

As one might expect in a high-octane organization captained by a guy with equal parts of ideas, brains, and courage, moving at the speed of a Falcon-20 jet, people were expected to meet a very high bar. Yet, the quickest ticket out of that organization went not to managers who missed performance targets, but to those who misused their position by treating others with disrespect. The first strike in that zone got you gone, because Smith was prescient enough to realize that people who can't fully trust or respect their leader aren't going to go all-out for that person, and all-out was exactly what it took to make FedEx work.

But it doesn't end there, because people everywhere perform so much better when they don't have to question motives, find hidden intent, or slow down to make absolutely certain that they don't make any mistakes.

Rather than treat moral clarity and persuasion purely from an academic perspective (which he is capable of doing), Roy patiently, and with wonderfully clear, crisp real-life examples obtained through nearly three decades of research, teaching, and practicing these behaviors, walks the reader through the business case and then down the path to capturing the exceptional power of moral leadership. Not just because it's the right thing to do, but also because, as Fred Smith had figured out, it's also the profitable thing to do.

Read it and reap!

Bill Catlette
founding partner, Contented Cow Partners

Introduction

Leadership in a word is influence. For the purposes of this book it is influence that leads to the realization of a positive vision that otherwise would have been deferred or never realized. Some of us have been fortunate enough to feel the strong gravitational pull of a leader that compelled us to lose ourselves in the pursuit of a noble vision and mission, and in the process accomplish more than we ever dreamed possible. My experience with such leaders at FedEx (Fred Smith, Judith Rogala, Steve Friedrichs et al.) had profound personal and professional implications that extended far beyond the great business success story of FedEx and the years I was fortunate to spend in leadership roles there.

It is my intent to illustrate the internal psychological system (our "soular system") that produces this leadership influence in a way that captures what Oliver Wendell Holmes Jr. called

1

the "simplicity beyond complexity." That is, to go beyond naive simplicity or needless complexity to the heart and foundation of effective leadership. These principles are relatively straightforward to understand, but hard to practice because of our self-inflicted moral and psychological damage. My goal is to share insights that will make effective leadership a natural extension of who you are, while ensuring that your ability to influence others grows with every decision and action. In addition, these principles will help you develop greater emotional intelligence, inner peace and a natural state of mindfulness that will significantly enhance your ability to build and sustain effective relationships, whether personal or professional.

In part, this book is also a reaction against the tendency to view leadership and organizations primarily through the lens of social science constructs that, while certainly of value in some cases, do not address the foundational intersection of human nature and effective leadership: an understanding of which is increasingly absent in leaders at all levels according to a large body of research and public surveys. The academic tendency to dissect any subject into more micro and discreet parts contributes to this trend, as is evident in the prevailing focus on emotional intelligence over the past two decades. Of course emotional intelligence is critical to leadership, but a micro focus (e.g., on the limbic system and amygdala) has produced an emphasis on the reactive "management" of emotions, when a more proactive approach that naturally creates positive emotions, while eliminating unhealthy ones, is possible with a macro understanding of our entire and highly integrated psychological system. In a postmodern society which has simultaneously diminished the importance and objectivity of ethics and morality, these trends have fueled the rise of disciplines and leaders that continue to dissect us and focus more attention on our differences than the common universal values upon which profound and enduring influence must be built.

This is intended to be a practical work with immediate relevance and value. While there are citations in this book where appropriate, the internal dynamics of our moral and psychological systems do not lend themselves to pure empirical research. Thus, I have based the content of this book on universal principles that, while validated by credible research, should also be self-evident to readers from their life experiences. These principles are presented within the framework of models and related exercises that have produced what has typically been characterized as "life-changing" impact by those who have participated in our leadership development programs. While our full experiential approach cannot be replicated in a book, I believe you will find valuable insight in what has been reproduced within these pages.

Given the low levels of trust and engagement well documented in many of our organizations, nothing is more relevant or compelling in the current discussion of leadership than how to become a person others trust and respect. Especially in our increasingly volatile, uncertain, complex and ambiguous world and operating environments, these fundamental areas of character are where the primary leverage exists for increased influence, engagement and performance. Few, if any among us, would follow a leader into an uncertain future absent a deep trust in their character and integrity, no matter their level of knowledge or expertise. No wonder so many "leaders" are continually looking back over their shoulder to see if anyone is actually following, even more costly behavior when the future is changing so rapidly right in front of them.

It is futile to expect those we presume to lead to take risks, innovate, fully invest themselves or act in alignment with publicly articulated cultural values without this strong foundational base of trust and respect. What we can expect absent this foundation are hesitation, delays and failures in execution, CYA behavior driven more by unwritten rules than by the values hung on office walls, and communication "up the chain" which bears little relationship to reality, producing poor strategic decisions as a result. For in spite of all the focus on change the foundational element in the leadership equation remains constant: human nature and the traits which inspire others to follow.

Only leaders who continually increase their integrity, by recognizing and correcting their unconscious moral blind spots, can elicit the trust and respect of others that is required to produce cultures characterized by open communication, continuous learning, innovation, faster execution, discretionary effort, higher quality and thus exceptional performance results. It may seem paradoxical, as is often the case with the simplicity beyond complexity, that leadership producing high levels of trust, respect and influence is easier to develop than the converse. However, this transformational leadership influence simply requires the self-awareness, along with an effective process, that enables us to improve our inner alignment and integrity with each decision and action. The converse requires enormously stressful and energy depleting psychological processes that slowly destroy the leader along with the organization.

Finally, I have tried to write a lean book, trusting you the reader to grasp concepts and make practical application without excessive verbiage from me. I have also cited numerous articles and research in key areas you may wish to further explore.

I deeply appreciate you taking this journey with me to explore how we can deepen and extend our leadership influence, while increasing our emotional intelligence and inner peace, by understanding and aligning our internal moral and psychological system.

Overture

No Country for Old Men

Book by Cormac McCarthy. Oscar-winning screen adaptation by the Coen brothers.

Llewelyn Moss is twisting and turning in bed, unable to sleep, because he forgot to give a drink of water to a dying man. He came upon a drug deal gone bad in the West Texas desert while hunting earlier that day, and found a number of dead guys lying around after an obvious shootout. One guy sitting in a pickup truck, however, was still alive though critically injured. "Agua," he begged Llewelyn in a whisper, "Agua for God's sake."

Llewelyn forgot to find some water for the dying man because he became obsessed with finding the money from the drug deal gone awry. But now his conscience is not buying his rationalizations for his screwed-up priorities, so unable to sleep, he gets up in the night to take some water to the man he earlier neglected.

The lessons?

We waste precious time and add much self-induced stress when we ask our moral conscience to compromise…because it won't. We doom ourselves to years of guilt and countless futile attempts to rehash and rationalize past behavior when we fight our moral compass. Why? Because it doesn't buy fiction.

If we come to our senses and try to do the right thing later, circumstances will have changed, the original impact of doing the right thing will be mitigated, and unintended consequences are likely to occur. When Llewelyn returns to the scene the man is already dead, and he leaves clues that later lead not only to his death, but to the death of his wife also. Delaying or deferring doing the right thing usually results in a lot of unexpected and unpredictable collateral damage.

Moral leaders keep their hearts pure so their minds will be clear and present, so they will not betray the trust of others, and so they can sleep well at night.

Recognizing the "forever" implications of each moral step, no matter how small, is not a burden, it's liberating. We are freed from the stress of constantly calculating if and when we should compromise, and from all the lasting guilt and consequences if we do.

PART 1

OUR SOULAR SYSTEM

CHAPTER 1

The Heart
of Moral Leadership

O n the evening of April 10, 1865, just four days before
his death, a crowd of about 3,000 gathered outside
of the White House calling for some words of victory and
celebration from President Lincoln. Lee had just surrendered
at Appomattox and America's long, bitter and costly Civil War
was finally over. It would seem only natural for any leader to
be swept up in the joy and relief of the moment and respond
as the crowd expected with a rousing victory speech. It would
also seem quite the rational and politically expedient response
for Lincoln to reinforce the role his leadership had played in
saving the Union from its darkest hour and greatest challenge.

Lincoln, however, as was often the case, responded with
a completely unexpected and unconventional decision. His

decision was not emotionally driven by the moment, nor was it produced from the rational process that many leaders would use to calculate the risk versus rewards to their popularity and future success. It was a decision prompted by his higher moral voice, a voice he had long exercised and strengthened so that his rational and emotional dimensions were subordinate and aligned to support his moral compass.

Rather than be emotionally or rationally driven in his response to the crowd, President Abraham Lincoln quickly removed himself entirely from the scene at a time when most leaders would take center stage and full credit. Instead, he gave a special request to the Marine band: "I have always thought 'Dixie' one of the best tunes I have ever heard," he said. "It is good to show the rebels that with us they will be free to hear it again."

In what the President could have understandably perceived as an insignificant moment, after so many life and death decisions during the war, his emotional and rational dimensions were still naturally subordinate to his higher moral dimension due to a lifetime of training and practice. He not only recognized within a 24-hour period that his leadership role needed to shift dramatically from winning a war to uniting a divided nation, but how the smallest of decisions could serve or detract from that noble vision. Remarkably, he required no meditation break, no extra time to weigh his options, nor did he feel the need to consult with advisors before immediately making a profoundly insightful decision.

How does this morally exceptional and insightful leadership become so natural and intuitive? It comes from the refusal to compromise the Golden Rule and our integrity in the smallest of decisions and moments. With us, as was said of Lincoln, it requires the discipline to recognize and consider the moral implications of every thought, decision and action. It is this discipline that produces a healthy and aligned psychological system where our higher moral voice is continually exercised and strengthened to produce moral clarity, healthy rational and emotional processes, and thus effective decisions and behavior as a natural and unconscious outcome.

Introduction to our Soular System

I've named this internal psychological system that drives our thoughts, decisions, communication and behavior our soular system because "soul" typically refers to a fundamental animating force. This internal system that animates our thoughts and actions has three dimensions: moral, rational and emotional. I have yet to meet someone who is not able to distinguish these dimensions, or voices, which speak to us and prompt us to think and behave in ways that either increase or diminish our relationship and leadership effectiveness.

Based on our decisions, communication and behavior over time, we exercise and strengthen one of these dimensions more, thus placing it in the central, or leadership role of our soular system. The primary influence of each of these dimensions on our thoughts and behavior, when placed in that central leadership role, may be defined as:

1. Higher Moral Dimension: Our moral compass or conscience, the internal voice that asks: "Is this right?" The "heart" of a healthy soular system with a focus on how to achieve the highest good, over the long-term, for all those affected by our decisions and behavior.

2. Rational Dimension: Our cerebral calculating function, the internal voice that tries to eliminate uncertainty and undesirable consequences by asking "Does this make sense?"

3. Emotional Dimension: The internal voice that asks, "How will this make me feel?" with the focus on me and this moment in time when leading our soular system.

Integrated Soular System

People ⟪   ⟫ Culture

Influence of System is Inside-Out

14

Disintegrating Soular System

People >>>   <<< *Culture*

Influence of System is Outside-In

Ideally these dimensions are aligned and integrated under the leadership of our higher moral voice, so that they produce the decisions and behaviors that elicit trust and respect from others, and thus influence them in positive ways. For when our moral dimension is at the center of our soular system, it exerts a strong gravitational pull that aligns our rational and emotional dimensions in supporting roles that enhance our influence, increase our critical thinking and decision-making capabilities, and improve our emotional intelligence and health. Our rational dimension is freed up from the neural storms created when we attempt to rationalize wrong behavior, so that there is an abundance of cerebral "free space" to think more critically and creatively. And rather than being overloaded with the toxic emotions that are created from trying to justify what we know to be wrong, our emotional dimension is free to create the healthy and positive emotional fuel required for our continual growth and success.

When these dimensions are not properly aligned and integrated under the leadership of our higher moral voice, however, this psychological system becomes increasingly fragmented and dis-eased as our rational and emotional voices begin to compete for a leadership role they are neither designed for nor qualified to assume. The internal conflict and stress generated as our moral voice becomes weaker from lack of exercise weakens the entire system and means that we, and our future, become increasingly influenced and shaped by our environment. We become reactive to people and circumstances rather than proactively influencing them, and increasingly perceive ourselves as a victim, the very antithesis of an effective leader.

In Part 2 of this book we will explore and illustrate in more depth how our internal soular system works either to erode or increase our leadership influence, emotional intelligence and inner peace. In Part 3 we will outline additional practical steps we can take to build a healthy, aligned and integrated soular system, not only within ourselves, but also within our teams and organizations. For now, let's focus on what constitutes our higher moral voice, or conscience, and how we may tap into the tremendous and oft neglected power it has to offer.

Our Higher Moral Dimension: Leader or Subordinate?

> *"The truth of the matter is that you always know the right thing to do. The hard part is doing it."*
> —General Norman Schwarzkopf

16

While there is a large body of research establishing that common universal moral values exist,[1] the research of the social scientist Shalom Schwartz is generally regarded as the most exhaustive and empirically validated in this area.[2] By "values" Schwartz refers to our beliefs as to what actions and related outcomes are most desirable; in other words, the standards by which we evaluate everything else, including the appropriateness of any norms, attitudes, traits, or virtues. Schwartz demonstrated that humans admire and aspire to the same higher moral values irrespective of national, cultural, racial, or socio-economic differences.

The priority order of these values is remarkably consistent across all societies, with the top two values, benevolence and universalism, described as "self-transcendence." Of the ten values Schwartz found to be universal only one with a personal focus, self-direction, appears in the top five, and it is strongly associated with self-transcendence, as it describes the personal freedom required to chart one's own higher and meaningful course in life. Because these self-transcendent values are so universally admired they have the power to elicit the deepest trust and respect from others. Thus, they are the foundational values and moral voice, or "heart"

These self-transcendent universal values, which our higher moral voice prompts us to follow, may be essentially summarized in two fundamental principles: the Golden Rule for behavior and Integrity in communication.

in our soular system, and affect our ability to influence others far more than any knowledge or skill we may possess. In fact, if our decisions and behavior do not consistently reflect these self-transcendent values, any other special knowledge or expertise we may have is essentially irrelevant to our leadership endeavors, as we will neither be trusted nor respected enough for others to follow where we presume to lead them.

The Golden Rule

The case for the Golden Rule as the essence of these universal values, and thus the voice of our higher moral dimension, is compelling in both the scientific and religious literature.[3] Integrity in communication is of course a component of the Golden Rule, but due special consideration given its impact on our trustworthiness and ability to influence others. While we may encounter a few scenarios in our lifetime where not disclosing the full truth may be the best application of the Golden Rule, anytime we lie or distort the truth we do significant damage to our inner psychological system and thus reduce our future leadership influence, as we will discuss later in detail.

The Golden Rule, as it is generally known in the West, is: "So in everything, do to others what you would have them do to you, for this sums up the Law and the Prophets" (Matt. 7:12 NIV). This brief statement from Jesus, present in kind in every major religion, is much deeper and more profound in implication than may appear at first look. It is helpful to consider its full implications vis-à-vis Kant's categorical imperative: "Act only according to that maxim whereby you can, at the same time, will that it should become a universal law."[4] In essence the Golden Rule requires us to regard the long-term consequences for all those affected as the primary consideration in our decisions and actions.

I have read a few authors who contend that the Golden Rule cannot be effectively applied to leadership. One cited the example of a leader who enjoyed parties and happy hour informal meetings, but whose employees found them ineffective intrusions into their personal time. The conclusion: you can't be an effective leader by treating everyone as you would like to be treated. This is an inappropriate and shallow interpretation of the principle, as is evident from simply considering its final words... "for this sums up the Law and the Prophets."

The Golden Rule is an executive summary of the higher universal principles required for effective human relationships, civil societies and influencing others. "Love your neighbor as yourself" is another common quote from Jesus that he also described as the essence of the Law and Prophets. It should be clear that these statements have nothing to do with parties and other such relatively trivial considerations. They ask us to care enough for others to do what is in their long-term best interest, because that is how we would wish to be treated. In the case of the leader who enjoyed happy hour with his employees, the Golden Rule would require of him to consider how he would wish to be treated if he were an employee and had higher priorities such as family after normal working hours.

Nor is the Golden Rule primarily about being "nice" to others, although that is how it is often defined in our culture. That aspect only scratches the surface. Which one of us would prefer that someone be "nice" to us in order to spare our immediate feelings, but at the expense of our long-term growth, success and happiness? Yet how often do we "do unto others" precisely that? There is a way to speak and act in the best interest of others, yet with deep care and empathy, that captures the essence of the Golden Rule. It is a relatively straightforward and simple principle to understand, but one that is very hard to practice if we have not aligned and exercised our inner soular system to produce it as a natural outcome.

Confucius made the Golden Rule a centerpiece of his philosophy in one of the most ancient versions in recorded history. When asked, "Is there any one word that could guide a person throughout life?" he replied, "How about 'shu' [reciprocity]: never impose on others what you would not choose for yourself?" (Analects XV.24). He continued, "The humane man, desiring to be established himself, seeks to establish others; desiring himself to succeed, he helps others to succeed. To judge others by what one knows of oneself is the method of achieving humanity."

It was his unwavering commitment to the Golden Rule that enabled Lincoln to have such clarity in thought, decisions and communication on the then contentious issues of slavery and succession. Speaking in Cincinnati in February of 1860, President-elect Lincoln echoed Kant and Jesus when he said: "I hold that while man exists, it is his duty to improve not only his own condition, but to assist in ameliorating mankind; and therefore, without entering upon the details of the question, I will simply say, that I am for those means which will give the greatest good to the greatest number."[5] In no statement was Lincoln's commitment to the Golden Rule more unequivocal or compelling than when he wrote, "As I would not be a slave, so I would not be a master."[6]

Lincoln's thought process on what were, at the time, confusing and complex issues to many illustrates the simplicity beyond complexity that Oliver Wendell Holmes Jr. dreamed about. For many leaders there are confusing and ostensibly complex issues in our postmodern culture that pose daunting challenges. When we address those later in this book, please keep in mind the clarity of thought and insight that Lincoln's approach brings to such issues, as there is no issue or scenario so challenging or complex that the same thought process will not yield clarity as to where the moral high ground lies.

Lincoln, Confucius, Jesus and Kant understood what seems lost on many leaders in our "advanced" culture: that when one behaves and communicates from the higher moral ground, the vast majority of people will not only reciprocate in kind, but be influenced to create a pay-it-forward domino effect throughout the organization. If, however, we operate from a lower plane, we should not be surprised to see corrupted communication and behavior driven by narrow self-interest reflected in our teams and organizational cultures. This law of

Leaders who understand the natural law of stimulus and response know that if they look in the mirror and change their own behavior, rather than first point a finger of blame, that change in stimulus will produce a different and higher response in others.

reciprocity is a fundamental tenet of human nature that we violate at our own peril. It is why some leaders find their pleas and directives for others to change often met with indifference or even active resistance.

Workforce reductions have provided many useful illustrations of how the Golden Rule can be applied in very challenging scenarios...or more often not applied. If management were relatively certain that your position would be among those eliminated in an effort to save the business, would you prefer them to remain quiet to spare you emotional pain and surprise you at the last moment with the news, eliminate your job immediately to free you up, or inform you well in advance of your release date, giving you time to search for other employment? What one would initially consider emotionally "nice" in the present moment is not the same decision and behavior that would result from a thoughtful application of the Golden Rule.

February 4th, 2019, "Black Monday" at GM, was the beginning of a workforce reduction of about 14,000 factory and white-collar workers in the U.S. A spokesperson for GM refused to confirm any exact numbers or dates for the reduction just one week prior because "our employees are our priority" and "we want them to be informed first." They demonstrated exactly what they meant by "priority" and "informed" when hundreds of staff in corporate offices, some with over two decades of service to GM, were called into conference rooms to be notified of their termination for the first time, then escorted out of the building half an hour later by extra security personnel.

One of these "priority" employees posted the following online: "Whole thing only took about 20 minutes. Turned in my laptop and badge and headed straight to the closest bar. Had lunch and now am drinking heavily. Expect to stay here until they close. Turned off my phone. Not a good day." How does one even begin to calculate the long-term consequences to these employees and their families from such a process?

Given the Golden Rule takes into account the long-term impact on all those affected by our decisions and behavior, in this case it would also include the effect on those employees remaining at GM and the longer-term health of the company. It seems obvious that the remaining GM employees would feel greater fear and uncertainty about their future employment and relative worth to the company. Indeed, it's hard to imagine that those feelings would not affect their engagement, productivity and quality of work for years to come. In fact, the concerns which led to the subsequent 2019 extended strike of 48,000 UAW worker at 50 GM plants, costing the company nearly $2 billion in production, were clearly tied to an increasing loss of trust in leadership. As this revised and expanded version of my book is being written in October of 2023, the extended implications of GM's Black Monday scenario remain quite evident and compelling amidst another labor dispute. The consequences of applying or failing to apply the Golden Rule in leadership last for generations in both families and organizations.

GM just happens to be in the news with such moves given their scale, but of course countless other similar examples could be given from other organizations. In contrast, I was fortunate to gain leadership experience at FedEx, a company renowned for its "People First" culture (which is important to distinguish from a "person" first culture). In over a decade of my work there, not a single employee was furloughed, though sometimes individuals experienced short-term reductions in hours or deferred pay increases in the best interest of all FedEx employees.

Fred Smith's devotion to the Golden Rule and People First culture was never more clearly demonstrated than in 1986, when he decided to discontinue the company's ZapMail initiative. This resulted in a substantial financial write-off and the immediate redundancy of 1,300 workers, not a single one of whom was furloughed. The impact of this philosophy, reflected over decades of balanced and sustained performance, speaks for itself. It is this foundational leadership philosophy that has resulted in FedEx's perennial recognition as one of the top 10 most admired global companies, as well as numerous best employer awards.

If we position our rational or emotional dimension as the leader and strongest voice in our soular system, it is easy to see how GM leadership had a very different perspective from the one I experienced at FedEx. It certainly "made sense" (was safer, easier, and less expensive, all shorter-term rational considerations) and was also far less emotionally challenging and painful to GM leadership for them to communicate and execute the process in the quick and clean way that they did. GM certainly, however, had the financial resources to support a very different process given it had posted a net profit of over $8 billion USD the prior year.

It is only when we follow our higher moral voice, based on universal values, that even from disparate viewpoints we can find the common higher ground that produces the best long-term results for all affected. It should be self-evident that "all affected" includes you as a leader, unless you wish to spend much of your life's remaining energy in futile attempts to rationalize actions that you knew to be wrong at the time.

Integrity

> *"...in looking for people to hire, you look for three qualities: integrity, intelligence, and energy. And if you don't have the first, the other two will kill you."*
> — **Warren Buffett**

Integrity (honesty and transparency) in communication is also ostensibly lacking in this GM scenario, as the entire process conflicts with the public words that GM considers its employees a top priority. These integrity gaps have become all too common, however, in part because we often think of integrity in communication, and the trust it produces, in terms of degrees. But if others do not have full trust and confidence that we will speak the truth and do the right thing without exception, then their skepticism, to whatever degree, will produce costly hesitation and delays in execution. The associated lack of respect for our character, even if diminished by only a few "degrees," will also eliminate the motivation and discretionary effort required for the highest quality of performance.

The seriousness of a "small" integrity violation is addressed by Marshall Goldsmith, author of *The Earned Life* and other best-sellers, when he wrote in his newsletter that…

> *"I do not coach people with integrity issues. I read an article in Forbes once that I found very disturbing. It was about people who, instead of being fired for ethics violations, got coaches. My personal belief is that people who commit integrity violations should be fired, not coached. Ask yourself, how many integrity violations does it take to ruin the reputation of a company? Just one. You don't coach integrity violations. You fire them."*

Marshall is in good company with Fred Smith, founder and CEO of FedEx, who unequivocally stated in the first talk I heard him make to new frontline managers that there was no second chance for integrity violations at FedEx.

Many of you understand why such renowned and influential business leaders have zero tolerance for a lack of integrity.

That is likely because you have worked in cultures character-ized by a lack of integrity, witnessed the absence of trust and the presence of fear it produces, and the related performance implications. Eventually what happens on the frontline in these organizations gets "massaged" so much in communica-tion that by the time it arrives at the executive suite it bears little resemblance to reality. Senior leaders make poor deci-sions based on this flawed information, further eroding the already low trust in leadership, and thus ensuring that even less of the truth is communicated in the future. This self-perpetuating cycle continues until you have a lifeless culture absent of conflict, confrontation or collaboration. People have their heads down in CYA mode, trying to avoid being blamed for the downward spiral in results, even though everyone has colluded to make it inevitable.

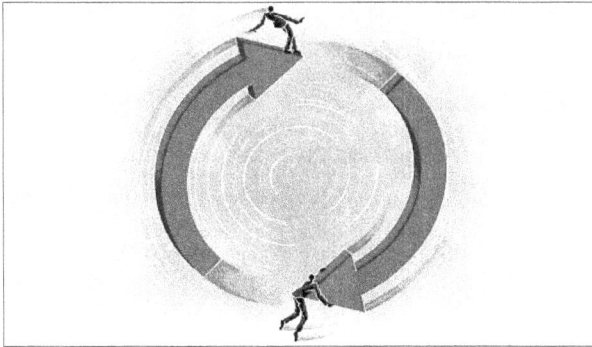

While the root cause of this cycle is typically the lack of the Golden Rule and integrity in leadership behaviors and communication, ultimately most everyone effectively cooper-ates to perpetuate this culture. How? By telling "white lies,"

each of them insignificant if we think of integrity in terms of degrees. No one is telling egregious falsehoods, just withholding some of the truth here, spinning it a little there, or remaining silent and feigning agreement.

Each person views these "small" violations of integrity as completely rational and justified for career purposes, and of course they also avoid the short-term emotional discomfort that integrity would require. They continue down this "harmless" and completely justified path until their moral compass is so corrupted that any communication skills they have developed are best suited only for survival in such toxic cultures. People have willingly, though often unconsciously, participated in the gradual erosion of their moral compass and authority until no one is influenced by what they have to say. It has been my experience in these scenarios that everyone conveniently has someone else to blame for this sorry state of affairs, so incredibly, no one is really responsible for arriving at this sad end point.

Absence of the Golden Rule in behavior and integrity in communication is how leaders begin the process of creating toxic cultures, leaving whatever positional power they may have as their only remaining mechanism for influence. People may act in minimal compliance to preserve their job because of positional power, but this requires the leader to constantly look back over their shoulder to see if anyone is actually following, then retreat to try and rally the troops, thus wasting enormous energy and time dealing with the inevitable consequences of their lack of moral leadership. Such dynamics ensure progress far short of the speed required in today's markets, and an almost certain dead end or fatal crash given the leader's backward focus: a focus demanded by the very culture they created.

The Current State of Moral Leadership

The Ethics Resource Center (ERC) entitled its 2011 report "Workplace Ethics in Transition," indicating a shift unlike any seen in prior surveys, and a prediction that has been validated by subsequent research. ECI's (Ethics & Compliance Initiative) 2018 Global Business Ethics Survey found that 16% of employees experienced pressure to compromise standards, which was a 23% increase over the prior survey and reflected an ongoing trend over the last decade. The ECI survey also found that only one in five employees indicated their company had a strong ethical culture, while 40% of those surveyed believed their organization's culture to be ethically weak.[7]

Revisiting the ECI global survey in late 2023 for the second edition of this book provides essentially the same picture and egregious gaps in ethics.[8] In summary the 2023 survey found that:

- The percentage of employees who feel pressure to compromise ethical standards remains essentially unchanged at 28%.
- The percentage of employees who observed ethical misconduct reached an all-time high of 65%.
- Retaliation against those reporting misconduct remains high at 46%.

- An alarming 87% of employees reported that they do not work in a strong ethical culture.
- On the encouraging side, the percentage of employees who reported observed ethical misconduct rose from 68% in 2020 to 72%.

The Edelman Trust Index has long illustrated how pervasive this lack of ethical behavior and related trust in leadership is across all our institutions. The trust barometer continues to reflect what Edelman describes as a crisis in leadership, stating that "In fact, none of the societal leaders we track—government leaders, CEOs, journalists and even religious leaders—are trusted to do what is right, with drops in trust scores for all."[9]

In LRN's 2019 "The State of Moral Leadership in Business" report, a striking 87% of respondents believed that the need for moral leadership is now greater than ever. Only 7% said that their leaders consistently demonstrated moral leadership, and an alarming 59% thought their leader exhibited few, if any, moral leadership behaviors. 83% believed their leaders would make better decisions if they based those decisions on the Golden Rule. There are clear performance implications in this research, as 94% of those who led with moral integrity and authority were viewed as effective in reaching their business goals, compared to only 14% of leaders who did not exhibit moral leadership.[10]

The impact of moral leadership on performance results is equally clear by looking at the leadership values and practices of companies that perennially appear on "Most Admired" and "Best Employer" lists, along with the balanced and sustained results they achieve in key people, service, quality and financial metrics. The performance implications of moral leadership should come as no surprise given that the number one factor contributing to a loss of meaning and purpose at work is when leaders ask others to act in conflict with universal higher values.[11] To request people to set aside these values is asking the impossible, so when they succumb to management pressure and act in conflict with these universal values, they suffer from significant guilt and stress that consumes their psychic energy and renders them AWOL even when present. To ask people to suppress their moral values and expect anything other than high levels of cynicism, skepticism and disengagement in response is the absolute height of leadership folly.

All this research supports what we intuitively know, that in most cases it is lower moral behavior by leaders that is at the root cause of lower engagement and performance in our teams and organizations. Leaders should not underestimate the powerful stimulus they introduce into an organization through their example, as it is a natural law that the behavioral response of others will reflect this stimulus. The only way to get a higher response in engagement and performance is to lead from the higher plane of moral character and integrity. Otherwise you can expect with 100% certainty to have a culture driven primarily by unwritten CYA rules rather than by the lofty values articulated by senior executives. And if that is the case, it's time for leadership to look in the mirror, as no new program, reorganization or consulting intervention can circumvent this natural law of stimulus and response in human behavior.

> *"Every great leader is, first and foremost, a good person."*
> — **Harry Flaris, Founder & CEO of Inspiration with Flair Consulting Services**

Many volumes have been filled with examples of leaders that violated the two universal moral values of the Golden Rule in behavior and integrity in communication. From Ken Lay to Elizabeth Holmes to Carlos Ghosn they have paid incredibly high prices personally and professionally, while doing incalculable damage to others and their organizations. We can avoid paying even a fraction of their price by giving these two principles careful consideration beyond what is obvious and superficial. For in spite of all the focus on change, the foundational and most important consideration in the leadership equation remains constant: human nature and the traits which inspire others to follow. And the more uncertain and chaotic the environment, the more critical a strong moral foundation of character, integrity and trust for those who ask others to follow them into the turbulent winds of change.

> *"What we so sorely need today is to be reminded of the universal values that hold us all together as families, communities, organizations, and even countries,*

*for these facilitate the higher vision and cultural
harmony that can bind us together spiritually."*
— Dwight N. Hopkins, The Alexander Campbell
Professor, The University of Chicago

A Reflection of the Culture?

The current lack of moral leadership should not be
surprising when you take a look at the lack of integrity in our
culture, to include:

- Advertisements with marketing spokespersons that rave
  about products, services and even medicines they have
  never actually used.

- An NFL receiver faking a clean reception of a pass that
  first hit the ground. Thousands openly cheer this attempt
  to cheat, then boo the referee that makes the correct call.

- That 93% of 40,000 Americans admitted to lying regularly at work.[12]

- Research by Dr. Paul Elkman that on average people lie
  about three times in each ten minute conversation.[13]

- Research by Dan Ariely, the James B. Duke Professor of
  Psychology and Behavioral Economics at Duke University,
  who has written extensively on what he calls our "fudge
  factor," i.e. our remarkable ability to compromise our
  morality and integrity within acceptable limits that still
  allow us to see ourselves as honest and good people.[14]

This decline in integrity and moral leadership has occurred
commensurate with an attempt to position the individual,

rather than universal values, as the source of moral authority. Charles Taylor, in *Sources of Self* and also in *A Secular Age,* characterizes this shift as one from a world view where an individual finds meaning through understanding and conforming to universal values, to a belief that our deepest meaning comes primarily from one's individual expression of authenticity.[15] This worldview, the roots of which can be traced back to the writings of Kierkgaard, Nietzsche and other 19th-to-20th century philosophers, stands in stark opposition to the ancient wisdom of Aristotle, Confucius, Jesus et al. who taught that one's purpose was to conform to the highest forms of virtue in order to serve and advance a larger community of citizens, and that in serving this larger purpose one would also find the highest levels of meaning and fulfillment.

"Important principles may and must be inflexible."
—**Lincoln in his last public speech, April 11, 1865**

Our Source of Values

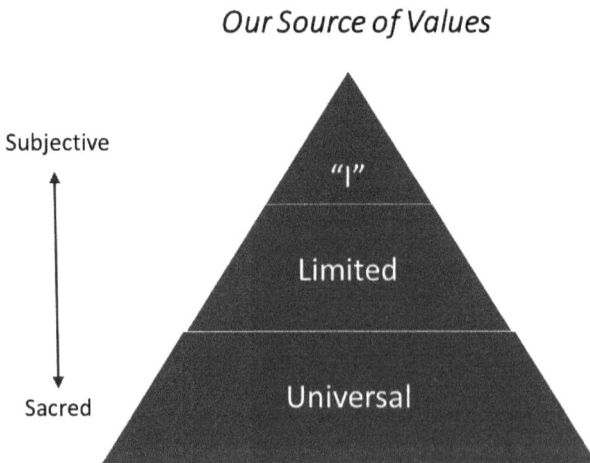

For most of human history mortals have understood that navigating long and challenging journeys required constantly orienting yourself using a fixed point like the North Star. Those who chose to navigate by their subjective feelings lie mostly buried under the sea or in unmarked graves. Children raised without any fixed points to navigate by often end up with the police or a psychologist, unconsciously seeking the limits that any mortal subconsciously recognizes as necessary to navigate the harsh realities of this world. The implications for adults attempting to navigate without fixed moral principles in societal and organizational cultures are no less painful, the process just tends to be more insidious and the consequences longer in appearing.

When a culture generally accepts a universal (sacred, divine) source as the ultimate basis for fixed and uncompromising values, or even a more limited but objective source (myths, traditions, etc.), there remains a consistent and coherent thread running through its beliefs and norms, and thus also through its leadership philosophy, priorities and practices. However, when we adopt a model that elevates individual feelings and perspectives ("my truth") as the highest source of values and meaning, then compromises in integrity and gaps in moral clarity inevitably appear with this increase in "flexibility." This shift explains in large measure the rise of emotions as a cultural focus, and the positioning by many of emotional intelligence as the singular most important leadership characteristic.

As feelings become elevated above fixed principles it is reflected in language, as it is now common to hear people say,

"I feel it is right (or wrong) to…," rather than to ground their perspective in something deeper and less subjective than feelings. And as language changes perceptions, both language and behavior reflect this shift, as in the expression "quiet quitting" and the related behavior now widely accepted. The language has been diluted to make it seem nearly benign, though there is nothing quiet about its effect either within the person (the guilt and stress of acting as an imposter), or upon their teammates and the organization. Neither does it remotely resemble quitting, since the person remains fully employed, so it might more accurately be characterized as loud lying.

Contrast this with the language of Lincoln in his second inaugural address, or his writing and speeches in general, in which he often referenced God, the Scriptures, and the eternal principles required for building free and civil societies. Contrast likewise his incredible leadership influence with that of many leaders today: influence so powerful because he was drawing from a deep and universal well of self-transcendent values that resonate within every human heart. Today such language is seldom heard, as someone might choose to be offended, and since individual feelings are the highest expression of authenticity, offense must be avoided even at the expense of objective facts and reality, as well as at the expense of one's ability to learn and succeed in the real world.

"With malice toward none, with charity for all, with firmness in the right as God gives us to see the right, let us strive on to

finish the work we are in, to bind up the nation's wounds, to care for him who shall have borne the battle and for his widow and his orphan, to do all which may achieve and cherish a just and lasting peace among ourselves and with all nations. "
—**Last sentence of Lincoln's 2ⁿᵈ Inaugural Address, March 5, 1865**

Lincoln's 2ⁿᵈ Inaugural Address, Lincoln in the center with papers in hand. (Library of Congress)

This cultural shift has significant implications for anyone trying to be a moral leader that can influence others, and for building healthy organizational cultures, which we will discuss in more detail later. For now it is worth reflecting on the fact that for leaders to improve reality, they must start with a clear and objective understanding of reality, rather than a perception colored by cultural influence or their feelings. They must also have the moral clarity and courage to help others likewise understand reality if they wish to influence them toward productive action. When leaders fail to appreciate these cultural shifts and realities, they produce profound unintended consequences, even from the most nobly intended decisions.

To appreciate the degree to which these consequences can occur within an organization, I recommend the article in Wired, describing three years of misery at the happiest company in tech.[16] Chaos seems a fair characterization of what the article describes in this organization's culture, and if one reads deeper beyond the bias in the article, the macro cultural shift we are discussing is readily apparent in its impact. To fail to appreciate this shift, and to allow its unfettered influence, can easily undermine any sense of strategic coherence and cultural cohesion in an organization, creating chaos and cultural disintegration just as happens within us when our emotions rule our soular system.

This cultural phenomenon happens two ways, "Gradually, then suddenly," as the character Mike in Hemingway's *The Sun Also Rises* replies when asked how he went bankrupt. Thus, a leader behind the curve of these dynamics can find themselves in a position where they are suddenly faced with such internal cultural chaos that recovery proves difficult and costly, if not impossible. Unfortunately, many leaders now seem to view this cultural shift through a low-resolution political lens, rather than through the higher resolution moral lens of what is best for the most people affected by their decisions and actions.

Instead of people-first cultures, accommodating this cultural shift has led to more person-first cultures where the loudest and most demanding voices of self-expression become the most important people to whom leaders respond with empathy and action. These leaders in most cases fail to appreciate the level of work involved to ascertain the true facts beneath the noise and thus the unintended consequences of their actions. They also tend to greatly underestimate the backlash from a silent majority of employees and customers, who do not appreciate them prioritizing individual self-expression (in the name of inclusion), ostensibly at the minimization or exclusion of the shared self-transcendent values proven to build and hold civil societies and healthy organizations together. This shift in priorities only serves to disenfranchise the vast majority of people who prioritize these shared values and who believe that pride should be earned through accomplishments and service to others, rather than celebrated because of identity or immutable characteristics.

Leaders also fail to appreciate how quickly this dynamic can cause their culture to disintegrate into such confusion and chaos that business strategy and execution becomes an afterthought. It is not, however, that difficult to predict nor avoid these "gradually then suddenly" disasters if you recognize the dangers of accommodating those loud voices that speak almost exclusively about their feelings rather than show a deep awareness of how their self-expression affects others. Leading from the higher moral ground by prioritizing the universal values that we all share is a proven formula based on exhaustive research as well as thousands of years of consistent human behavior and psychology. No strategy can succeed, or healthy culture be built and sustained, on any other foundation, no matter how politically or socially expedient it may seem viewed through the low-resolution political lens that many leaders appear to be looking through.

It may be worthwhile to consider the example of Martin Luther King Jr., who endorsed no political candidate or party, so that as he stated, he could be free to be critical of all on moral grounds. As we will discuss more later, his powerful and enduring influence resulted from him staking out the high ground of racial equality with such moral clarity and courage, anchored in universal moral principles, that he never vacillated or compromised his moral convictions. His influence was truly inside-out rather than the converse, and thus he never equivocated or was blown about with the loudest or richest political or social winds.

Capitulation to cultural trends ensures the absence of the moral clarity required to touch the deepest recesses of the human heart, where shared universal values are embedded, and thus precludes us from influencing others to any meaningful degree. So when leaders value and reward individual expression above the commensurate individual constraint required to enhance the whole, we should not be surprised to see the unraveling of a culture or organization into increasingly fragmented identities until the whole loses any meaning or power of cohesion. Effective leaders build a strong and sustainable foundation on what is common to us all (universal moral values), rather than fracture us based on individual self-expressions and superficial characteristics.

Yet, it seems reasonable to assume that most of us may have been influenced by this cultural shift to some degree. Is our soular system strong enough to resist these winds of change and shape lives and organizations with higher moral standards that compel others to follow? Is it realistic or worthwhile to try in the face of such popular resistance? To help us answer, let's look further at the example of Lincoln and the power of his influence.

CHAPTER 2

Abraham Lincoln: The Power of Moral Leadership

"Now, why was Lincoln so great that he overshadows all other national heroes? He really was not a great general like Napoleon or Washington; he was not such a skillful statesman as Gladstone or Frederick the Great; but his supremacy expresses itself altogether in his peculiar moral power and in the greatness of his character."
— Leo Tolstoy

"Every man is said to have his peculiar ambition, whether it be true or not, I can say for one that I have no other so great as that of being truly esteemed of my fellow men, by rendering myself worthy of their esteem."
— Abraham Lincoln, March 15, 1832

Lincoln's Example

To illustrate the nature, power and implications of moral leadership there is no better example than the man who has been consistently ranked as the most influential and best President in U.S. history, Abraham Lincoln. While other leaders have followed his legacy of moral and ethical leadership, historians are in remarkable agreement that no one in American history, before or since, demonstrated such moral courage in leadership with such profound consequences for our nation as Lincoln.

Abraham Lincoln was "a man of profound feeling, just and firm principles, and incorruptible integrity," wrote Civil War general and politician Carl Schurz.[17] "He was so modest by nature that he was perfectly content to walk behind any man who wished to walk before him. I do not know that history has made a record of attainment of any corresponding eminence by any other man who so habitually, so constitutionally, did to others as he would have them do to him. Without any pretensions to religious excellence, from the time he first was brought under the observation of the nation, he seemed, like Milton, to have walked 'as ever in his great Taskmaster's eye.'"[18]

"Any casual reader of Lincoln has to be struck by the consistency with which every argument, however technical or legal, or economic, took on moral dimension as well," wrote Lincoln scholar Stewart Winger.[19] Fellow attorney Samuel Parks wrote of him that "the great feature in Mr. Lincoln's character was his integrity in the longest sense of that term – his devotion to truth and justice and freedom in every department of human life and under every temptation. I have often said that for a man who was for a quarter of a century both a lawyer and a politician he was the most honest man I ever knew. He was not only morally honest but intellectually so – he could not reason falsely – if he attempted it he failed. In politics he never would try to mislead..."[20]

> *Abraham Lincoln could not reason falsely because he had trained his rational and emotional dimensions to be subordinate to his higher moral dimension; so much so that it became a natural and unconscious habit with him, just as it can with us.*

As already mentioned, Lincoln's reasoning on the contentious issues of succession and slavery were remarkably clear given the times and the perspectives of his peers. According to his own testimony he was already and always opposed to slavery by the time he began to show an interest in politics. His treatment of Frederick Douglas after several meetings prompted Douglas to state that "I was never more quickly or more completely put at ease in the presence of a great man than that of Abraham Lincoln."[21] In praising Lincoln for treating him as an equal Douglas mentioned how remarkable he found such treatment especially from someone who came "from a state with black laws." Lincoln's slavery stance and his treatment of black men and women as equals, given the culture and laws in the state he grew up in, illustrate just how impervious he was to outside-in influence due to his moral clarity.

One might say that Lincoln found it politically expedient to treat Douglas as an equal, but again, history shows that it was his higher moral voice that drove his behavior rather than a calculating (rationally driven) political consideration. Many other stories support this, including one from the fall of 1831 when Lincoln was only twenty-two years old. He was walking home from work when he met a black man (Haitian) named William de Fleurville. Striking up a conversation with him Lincoln learned that the man had been on his way to Springfield but had now exhausted his funds. That evening Lincoln campaigned among his fellow lodgers at his boarding house in New Salem to raise funds for the man and the next morning bid him farewell on his journey.

William de Fleurville had been trained as a barber and soon afterward opened the only barbershop in Springfield. After Lincoln moved to Springfield he frequented Billy the Barber's shop for the duration of the time he lived in Springfield, becoming not only a customer, but Billy's lawyer and lifelong friend. Lincoln continued to send messages to Billy after becoming President and likewise received letters in return, including one sent on New Year's Day of 1864 expressing hope that Lincoln would be reelected to a second term.[22] There was certainly no political consideration in the mix at the age of twenty-two when Lincoln took the time to talk to a young black man and go out of his way to help him. Any such considerations at the time and place would have, in fact, precluded him from even walking alongside in conversation with him.

It was not just Lincoln's understanding and practice of the Golden Rule that far exceeds the norm and stands in stark contrast to the culture of his day, but his high standards for integrity were no less exceptional. Perhaps no statement of Lincoln highlights his clarity about integrity, and differentiates his understanding and practice of it, than when in an 1846 letter he wrote, "I believe it is an established maxim in morals that he who makes an assertion without knowing whether it is true or false, is guilty of falsehood; and the accidental truth of the assertion does not justify or excuse him."[23]

How many people do you know who, like Lincoln, view the making of an assertion that is accidentally true, i.e., one made without full certainty and sincerity, the equivalent of telling a lie? If you want to calculate your odds of suffering from the worst kind of imposter syndrome, apply Lincoln's standard and take an inventory of everything you say to avoid conflict, appease others or advance your career that you do not deeply and sincerely believe or know to be true. Because in all those moments you are pretending to be someone that you are not. And since there is no vault in our unconscious where we can lock away the toxic feeling of being an imposter, eventually that feeling spills over into all our personal and professional relationships and efforts, eroding the foundation of self-esteem and confidence required for success in life and work. Because self-respect is a prerequisite to self-esteem, and no one respects an imposter.

To avoid this crippling syndrome Lincoln began early in life to pay attention to the guilt signals that make us feel weaker anytime we even think of speaking without full integrity. Signals that cause us to feel weaker because we are, in fact, becoming weaker psychologically and spiritually each time we violate the Lincoln standard. Likewise we become stronger each time we speak with full integrity and sincerity, no matter the immediate risk vs. reward calculations our rational dimension may try to insert or the immediate emotional discomfort.

The great internal psychological strength and resilience of Lincoln, due to this high standard of integrity, was what gave him the rare and unique combination of strong self-esteem and confidence combined with a compelling humility that endeared him immediately to so many people. While his humility and its leadership implications will be discussed more later in this book, it is worth carefully reflecting on the high level of integrity required to build the healthy self-respect, self-esteem and self-confidence required of any leader. Because no amount of hyperbolic self-talk, reading or coaching is more powerful than the unconscious prompting of our higher moral voice when we deserve to be reminded that we are a practicing imposter.

The depth and breadth of influence created by these high standards was well described by a local correspondent of the Chicago Tribune after meeting with Lincoln at Danville in

September, 1858: "...let a jury be empaneled from any part of our popular country, to try a cause, and they will take his exposition of the law and the facts of a case without a scruple; for they know that as Lincoln has never misconstrued the law, nor perverted the evidence, they can follow him and do no wrong. And when a man brings that kind of a reputation on the hustings, his power with the people is almost omnipotent."[24]

Lincoln's journey to exceptional moral character, integrity and almost omnipotent influence was, however, far from as straightforward and uneventful as some accounts present. In the winter of 1840 he fell into perhaps the darkest depression of his life, so much so that his friends feared for his life and confiscated any item which they thought he could use to commit suicide. Two events precipitated this descent into darkness, the first being his failure to deliver on his promise to the citizens of Illinois to greatly expand infrastructure within the state. During a third year of recession in the state many major transportation projects were halted, thousands of people lost their homes and many banks closed their doors.

The second event that contributed to the depth of his depression was his failure to keep his promise to marry Mary Todd. As her mercurial personality became more worrisome to him, and other events contributed to his belief that their marriage might be doomed, he reluctantly ended their engagement. The resulting public embarrassment for Mary Todd "kills my soul" he wrote, but of far more concern to him was the fact that he had broken his promise to marry her. About his ability to keep his word he wrote that "In that ability you know I once prided myself as the only or at least, the chief gem of my character." Until he recovered that gem of integrity Lincoln wrote that "I cannot trust myself in any matter of much importance."[25]

What did Lincoln do? For the financial debacle in Illinois he took full responsibility and informed the people of Illinois that he would be resigning at the end of his term. As to the breaking of his engagement, he viewed that as a significant moral failure despite all the compelling rational and emotional justifications available to him. He then took a decade to rebuild his personal and professional life after a long period of such dysfunction that he neither slept nor ate with any regularity. "I feel I must die or do better," he wrote to his law partner.

The impact of the years spent reflecting on his political and personal failures, and a deep resolve to exercise more care and diligence before either offering his ideas or making a promise, echoes through the halls of history. Over two decades later, when some began to doubt and publicly speculate on whether Lincoln had the courage to keep his promise to activate his Emancipation Proclamation on New Year's Day of 1863, Frederick Douglas responded by saying, "Abraham Lincoln will take no step backward. If he has taught us to confide in nothing else, he has taught us to confide in his word."[26]

What would you do, or have you done, in similar personal and professional scenarios? Many so-called self-esteem gurus and coaches today would advise you on how to release the guilt of those failures and wake up every day with the unbridled confidence that you are a near perfect creation in a world desperately in need of your ideas and leadership. How many of us would welcome such self-esteem and confidence, no matter how misplaced? Or how many of us, upon the failure to keep a single promise or failure in a singular responsibility, would spend as many years as required to reorder our values and priorities until valid self-esteem and self-confidence had been earned? Given the state of many organizations today and the world in general, despite no shortage of people enamored with their ideas and abilities, it would seem to be a question worthy of some reflection.

It was Lincoln's unwavering commitment to the highest standards of moral clarity and integrity, no matter the cost or how many years it took, that produced his exceptional ability to speak with penetrating and compelling words that reached deep into the hearts of his audience. From his responses to Stephen Douglas in the fall of 1854, his speech to the new Republicans from Illinois in 1856, to his speech in reaction to the Dredd Scott decision in 1857 the reactions to Lincoln were such that "When he concluded the audience sprang to their feet, and cheer after cheer told how deeply their hearts had been touched." The clarity and power in the structure and content of these speeches was the main ingredient in Lincoln's rise,[27] and to understand the cost he paid and the process he followed to achieve this exceptional moral clarity and courage is central for anyone wishing to approach his influence.

The gap between Lincoln's almost omnipotent influence with people and most of the influence (so-called) you see from many leaders today might be more accurately described as a chasm. Neither the reasons for that gap, however, nor the remedy is hard to understand. But to apply the remedy requires a remarkable depth of self-awareness about the health of our inner soular system, as well as a willingness to apply whatever medicine is required, for as long as needed, before we can begin to approach the levels of trust, respect and influence that Lincoln enjoyed.

Is It Worth It?

All of us in search of greater influence, more effective relationships and a deep inner peace would do well to think deeply on Lincoln's example. But in so doing we may understandably ask if this standard is worth the effort, or even realistic? The answer depends on how much you desire to shape your life and positively influence others, rather than become more reactive and a victim by choice of other people and circumstances. The positive power of moral influence is truly almost omnipotent, as was said of Lincoln, and as is fully born out in history. Whether it is "worth it" should be evident from the impact of moral leadership on the world and from our own personal life experiences.

For each of us, as with Lincoln, the pursuit of moral leadership is worth it because it enables us to:

- Intuitively and quickly produce moral clarity in the most challenging and complex situations, while others struggle with and delay strategic decisions.

- Increase our creative and critical thinking abilities by creating cerebral "free space" that guilt, stress and neural storms would otherwise occupy when we try to justify what we know to be wrong.
- Create healthy and positive emotions naturally from moral thoughts and actions. Eliminate the self-inflicted toxic emotions of guilt, bitterness, resentment and shame that we create when we blame others for our own choices. Continually reduce the need to reactively "manage" our emotions.
- Free us to be naturally present and mindful with others rather than constantly reliving past regrets or being distracted by the stress of current dilemmas. More present with others, less self-absorbed.

For our teams and organizations, moral leadership is worth it because it is an absolute prerequisite before people will:

- Communicate organizational realities rapidly and accurately so that fast and effective leadership decisions can be made. This level of communication and decision-making is the foundation of a learning culture, as opposed to a culture where unwritten rules ensure reality remains a highly guarded secret from those leaders who most need to know it.
- Act without the hesitation, skepticism and even sabotage that characterizes many teams and organizations. Faster execution is the result of full trust in leadership, while

executing at higher levels of effort and quality is a function of the respect that moral leadership elicits from others.

- Bring their full trust, loyalty, commitment and discretionary effort to work. These are attributes that reside only in the spiritual, higher dimension of others. It's not that there is a shortage of these qualities within the human heart today (as countless examples illustrate), but rather that there are too few leaders with the gravitational pull of moral character to touch and awaken these higher spiritual qualities in others.

> *"Work is contractual. Effort is personal. We give it up when, where, and for whom we choose."*
> — **Bill Catlette, author of** *Contented Cows STILL Give Better Milk*

The purpose of this book is to illustrate how we may develop Lincoln's level of moral integrity and leadership so that we may achieve these profound personal and professional results. It is not primarily to make a case for desiring to get there, although there will be some research cited and examples provided that should certainly increase your passion for the journey. But my intended audience is those who recognize that such a standard, however lofty, is certainly not too high given the enormous return on investment during our lifetime and beyond.

Is It Realistic?

Is it realistic for us to aspire to such a high level of moral character and leadership? Absolutely. As I mentioned in the introduction, the journey in the other direction is actually much more painful, and becomes increasingly more difficult, as one progresses along that path. As we explore how leaders successfully made the journey to high levels of moral leadership and influence it will become evident that the path is not nearly as daunting or difficult as may first appear, and that the payoff far exceeds the investment of time and energy required by a factor of magnitude that is impossible to calculate.

The answer to "is it realistic?" becomes even clearer when we recognize the reality that each one of us is already moving along one of two moral paths with each passing day. Every organic being or system is constantly growing or dying; there is no moral "status quo" that we can achieve and remain comfortably at for the rest of our lives. We are inevitably growing or dying a little in our moral character and integrity, and thus our influence, each day. Unfortunately, that growth or decay typically happens in such small increments that we often do not recognize either the path we have chosen, or its full implications, until years later when we start to reap the full consequences.

Consider this natural law of constant growth and decay as illustrated by these examples:

- Our universe is expanding (dying). We have already passed the golden age of star creation and the birth rate of stars continues to decline. Galaxies are being ripped away from each other at the speed of light (or greater), yet we remain billions of years away from the dark end.

Anyone of you notice these changes over the last few days…months…years?

- The same with our solar system, of course, since the sun is consuming a bit more of itself with each passing moment. So every day there is a bit less gravitational pull from the heart of our solar system, and as a result each year the earth is about 1.5 centimeters further away from the sun in its orbit. Do you recall the moment when you first looked up and recognized this change?

- Our physical bodies start to decline due to changes in the rate of cell creation vs. decay in our early twenties. I don't recall looking in the mirror on any day in my twenties, or for many years thereafter, and thinking "Oh my, today's the day, it's time to get serious." Do you?

In all three examples, though the changes are so small as to be indiscernible without careful examination, the consequences are lasting and profound. What a blessing it would have been to notice and understand the long-term implications of incremental changes at the cellular level in our early twenties. I certainly would have made some more proactive changes earlier in life, I suspect the same for many of you.

Yet, in the case of our internal soular system, we can indeed understand and recognize these daily incremental changes in either the growth or decay of our moral character and integrity. Thus, it is not at all unrealistic or daunting to continually increase the health of our soular system so that we enjoy daily increases in our influence, emotional intelligence and inner peace, with profound results and impact over the course of our lives. And we will explore precisely how to do that.

Given the compelling research, examples and practical implications of leading from our moral dimension and higher voice, it should be evident that we are designed for this dimension to be driving our thoughts, decisions and behavior. Whether you believe this wiring is the result of divine creation, or some other mechanism, practically all of us understand that both external influence and internal psychological health result when our higher moral voice is leading us. That premise is not only validated by extensive research, but by the consistent thread running through ancient philosophy and religion to the present. To place our moral dimension in a subordinate role to either our rational or emotional dimensions ensures not only that our higher voice becomes weaker from the lack of exercise over time, but that our rational and emotional dimensions become corrupted and lose their intended positive functions. The dire implications of this dynamic, along with the positive dynamics of a healthy and aligned soular system, will be further explored in Part 2.

CHAPTER 3

Our Rational and Emotional Dimensions

Our Rational Dimension: Subordinate or Leader?

Our rational decision-making process is associated primarily with our prefrontal cortex (PFC). The functions of the PFC in psychological terms are often described as executive functions, i.e., among other functions the ability to process information, options and conflicting thoughts in order to differentiate between the relative value of outcomes in our decision-making.

Our rational dimension must be feeling neglected in recent years, with all the focus on emotional intelligence, but there is evidence that especially among business leaders the rational voice remains a strong factor in thought and decision-making processes. In a study of 26,477 leadership program participants at the Center for Creative Leadership there was a clear majority and overrepresentation of Thinking and Judging preferences among leaders and managers (MBTI).[28] Michael Shadlen, MD, PhD, a principal investigator in Columbia's Mortimer B. Zuckerman Mind Brain Behavior Institute summarized his recent research by concluding that, "When we look hard under the hood, so to speak, we see that our brains are built pretty rationally, even though that is at odds with all the ways that we know ourselves to be irrational."[29] It is critical, therefore, that we understand the importance of this dimension, how it can be trained to support and enhance our moral and general leadership abilities, as well as how it can be corrupted.

When we choose to place our rational voice in the driver's seat, or center of our soular system, it attempts to analyze all the possible human responses and potential outcomes within our environment in order to produce a decision that makes the most sense given the relative risks and benefits. In other words, with regards to human relationships, it functions with the goal of minimizing error and variation and maximizing certainty. To state that objective, of course, is to immediately be struck by its futility with regard to human relationships and leadership.

In most of the examples leaders have shared in our sessions over the years it appears that our rational voice, when in the leadership role of our internal psychological system, often seeks what we consider to be a "safe" compromise between our moral and emotional dimensions. It attempts to calculate all the options, variables and possible reactions of others so that we can say or do what will avoid the most immediate emotional pain and egregious consequences, while also doing enough of the right thing to somewhat appease our moral compass. When we distort our rational voice's heathy function and position it as the leader of our soular system we are signing up for much greater stress and leadership ineffectiveness. Why? Because:

1. Given the number of stakeholders and people affected in a typical leadership (or even personal) decision, it is impossible to calculate all the potential combination of responses along with both the expected and unintended consequences. One would have to be essentially omniscient to do so, and we are not, thus we become trapped in a futile and enormously stressful process that consumes an inordinate amount of our time and psychic energy.

2. Even if we had the capability to process all this information effectively, we would be predicting potential human responses based on our prior experience, and given how unique and complex humans are, our predictions would certainly be wrong in a significant percentage of cases.

3. Our higher moral dimension does not compromise on the universal values of the Golden Rule and integrity in communication. We can't "almost" or "partially"

practice the Golden Rule or integrity in a scenario. Therefore, any attempt to rationalize a decision outside of these two principles will produce significant psychological stress and permanent damage to our soular system and leadership influence, as we will discuss in more detail.

4. Putting our rational voice in the driver's seat of our soular system means that the moral integrity of our words and actions will vary depending upon the circumstances, perceived risks and predicted outcomes. We will then be regarded, and correctly so, as inconsistent in character and unpredictable in behavior. Who will then grant us either the trust or respect required to have any meaningful leadership influence? Especially since the greater the uncertainty, the more important the integrity, consistency and strength of a moral leadership foundation before people will trust us enough to follow us into the turbulent winds of change.

"It is my purpose, as one who lived and acted in these days . . . to show how the malice of the wicked was reinforced by the weakness of the virtuous, how the councils of prudence and restraint may become the prime agents of mortal danger ... and how the middle course, adopted from desires for safety and a quiet life may he found to lead direct to the bull's-eye of disaster."
— **James B. Stockdale,**
Thoughts of a Philosophical Fighter Pilot

I reflected this management tendency to place our rational voice in the driver's seat of our soular system, choosing what I thought at the time to be a safe "middle" course, when I was a Managing Director responsible for hundreds of people and over 100M P&L. I had been in leadership roles for several years, received numerous awards and recognition, and certainly believed my higher moral dimension was generally in control of my soular system. Yet, unfortunately, I put my rational dimension in charge when I made a decision to avoid as much interaction as possible with a new corporate Officer to whom I reported.

I had already been warned that this person did not care for my leadership style, or some of my management personnel decisions, and was "out to get me." So on the day of their first visit to my operating area I made the fateful decision to send a staff member to pick them up at the airport, rather than do that personally. This would limit the time alone I had to spend with them, and thus minimize the risk of any undue conversation and potential conflict. And, of course, protect the leaders who reported to me from any negative consequences from the fallout.

This decision, a completely rational and well justified one in my mind, ultimately led to a stressful and unproductive relationship with my boss over the next year, and produced negative consequences that, had I made a higher decision, could have been avoided. While our operating area continued to produce good results, there is no way to calculate the lost opportunity cost to me for spending a year in unnecessary stress. Nor any way to calculate the cost of potential growth opportunities lost for those talented leaders who reported to me because I shifted into a self-protective survival mode.

Had I reflected on whether that decision exemplified the Golden Rule, by asking if it was in the best long-term interest of all those who would be affected by it (including me), the answer would have been self-evident. Yet it was not until years later that I reflected on this decision with the depth necessary to fully understand my decision-making process and its implications. Later we will further explore how formative experiences in my childhood predisposed my moral dimension to be hijacked in this scenario, and how you can identify those scenarios where the same process is likely to occur to you.

As the philosopher Immanuel Kant argued, if we do the right thing in a scenario because we have rationally calculated that the immediate consequences are favorable, our behavior has no moral worth or honor. Because the next calculation may produce a decision to lie or to do wrong. Kant used the example of a shopkeeper who decided not to shortchange a customer, but only because of the risk of losing other customers if they found out what he did. Nothing robs us of more time, joy, energy and peace than turning on our internal calculator to attempt the impossible task of predicting future reactions when we already know what the right thing to do is. How much of our life's precious energy are we willing to steal from ourselves?

Doing the right thing just because it is right is the secret to freeing up our psychic energy and cerebral space for learning and growth. This freedom from the toxic neural storms created by stress and guilt enables us to first think, and then communicate, with the same primary element that characterized Lincoln's speeches and writing, which was "*logos* – rational argument, logic, again clearly stated."[30] Thus, Lincoln's arguments and positions remain just as compelling in written as spoken form, as they did not depend upon emotionally laden content or personal charisma for their power to convict and persuade. This is an interesting point of contrast with much of the speech that characterizes our culture, as it seeks to compel by force of volume or sheer repetition rather than through intellectual rigor, and in fact, often seeks to prohibit the healthy and respectful debate of Lincoln's day that is required to produce such.

Our Emotional Dimension: Subordinate or Leader?

Unlike our rational dimension, our emotions and emotional intelligence (EI) have received extraordinary attention in recent years. Like many of you I am indebted to Goleman and Boyatzis for their seminal and valuable work in EI. However, given the now generally accepted importance and popularity of the subject, there has also arisen plenty of unsubstantiated hype that contradicts not only the best research, but human experience and common sense as well.

From some of the most popular business authors, TED speakers and faculty from leading universities, all internationally recognized, I have read that the amygdala is 35 times more powerful than the frontal cortex, that most adults are about 9 years old emotionally, that all of our decisions are driven primarily by emotions, and that we have little control over the emotions we feel in any given moment. These and other similar premises are then expanded to tell us how to better manage our emotions, as well as how to communicate and lead more effectively. Yet each of them is not only ostensibly false, and so proven by research, but used to create "solutions" that address neither the reality nor root causes necessary to help us become emotionally healthy, intelligent and resilient.

These speculative assumptions about our limbic system can produce a myopic focus that traps us in the reactive cycle of trying to manage our emotions, when there is a more proactive approach that eliminates the need for the constant management and correction of our emotional "elephant" (now popular analogy first used by psychologist Jonathan Haidt). This prevention-based approach enables us to stop trying to ride an unruly elephant, a challenging and draining task that requires constant corrective action, and instead lead a well-trained and powerful beast down a path that enhances both our psychological health and leadership capabilities. The alternative of placing our emotional dimension in charge of our inner soular system means that we are driven to say and do what feels best for me in this moment, absent little rational consideration, much less any long-term moral perspective. This is the antithesis of self-transcendence and the Golden Rule, as it is all about "me" and all about "now."

Some of the terms now prevalent around our emotions (hijacking, triggered, etc.) have been distorted from their original intent and reflect a cultural shift that seeks to absolve us of responsibility for our emotions. But anyone who grants others the power to control their emotions, and thus their related thoughts and actions, has officially achieved victim status and rendered themselves powerless to influence others or even to shape their own environment or future. Beyond that, such a person becomes increasingly self-absorbed and imprisoned on an emotional rollercoaster ride of their own construction: not someone most of us would choose to be around, much less follow.

Given this power of our emotions to enhance or cripple our leadership ability, there is certainly no shortage of advice on how to achieve emotional intelligence. In reviewing a large body of literature on the subject there are some clear themes that emerge, which may be summarized as: since most of the emotions you experience occur almost instinctively, you can't control how you feel in any given moment. But you can control how you react to those feelings. My question is this: Why would we choose to be more reactive rather than proactive, especially with something as powerful, for better or worse, as our emotions? Reactive implies lost time, lost opportunity, damage control and a lot of energy that could be directed more positively if we can reduce the need for the constant management of our emotions.

The costly problem with some of this popular thought on EI is that the focus is primarily on one part of our psychological system (limbic), with most of that attention focused on our amygdala. Joshua Greene (Harvard), or any credible psychologist or neuroscientist understands our cerebral and psychological processes as a system that is far more integrated and complex than is often presented in popular EI literature.[31] This system has intricate and often unconscious feedback loops that, if we fail to understand, produce severe unintended consequences. But as complex as it is, there are lessons from a systems perspective that we can apply to take a much more holistic and prevention-based approach to EI and leadership influence.

Understand the Entire System and Root Causes

Emotions do not appear out of thin air, nor are they the irresistible impulses of our "lizard brain" (the differences between the human brain and any lower life form are vast in scope and scale). Emotions are primarily the end-of-process outcomes of the conscious and unconscious interactions between our thoughts, our memories, environmental stimuli and our behavior. Imagine how complex and challenging it is to "manage" such a system after a few years of life experience and the incalculable number of feedback loops created between our past thoughts, memories, behavior and the meaning we attach to them. You might as well try driving while looking in your rear-view mirror.

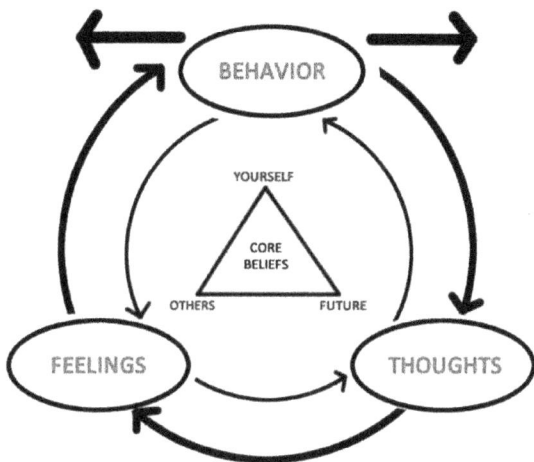

So what to do? From a systems perspective we can discover the simplicity beyond complexity that enables us to identify leverage points for creating a healthier system, instead of reactively trying to manage what is primarily a symptom of our psychological system's health...our emotions. But we must first move beyond a myopic focus on emotions to a more holistic and accurate understanding of the entire system.

Positive emotions are naturally produced from meaningful behavior; meaningful because it is of service to others. Emotions themselves do not produce meaning or happiness, nor can we create positive ones by chasing them with self-indulgent behavior. The best long-term path to creating positive emotions, and eliminating negative ones, is to increase the selfless value of our behavior to others. Our guaranteed ROI from this service orientation will be positive emotions to fuel more such meaningful behavior, along with memories and thoughts that keep our emotions positive and motivating. By introducing a healthier stimulus (more meaningful service to others) our psychological system must change; it's the natural law of stimulus and response. And the change will produce more positive and healthier feedback loops between our memories, thoughts and behavior, with healthier and more positive emotions as a natural result.

It has long been established that what fires together wires together in our synaptic processes. Most of us don't need to try to completely unravel the tangled unconscious web we have woven over our lifetime. We just need to continuously improve our psychological wiring by increasing our focus on service to others, and deepening the value of that service. The new firing patterns this creates will increasingly override the old patterns and naturally produce constant improvements in our psychological and emotional health. What we do in the present has great power to heal our past, often more than revisiting our past too often or too deeply in the effort to make sense of it... for there is often little sense to be found. Obviously there are exceptions in cases of severe or complex trauma, but even in such scenarios more proactive and future-oriented

We are better served by guiding our inner child on a path of growth, rather than one that, however unintentionally, further reinforces and enables its immature behavior.

forms of psychotherapy are proving remarkably effective at discovering and removing the root causes of such trauma.[32]

Understand Your Environmental Triggers and Responses

While we can never fully unravel the tangled web we humans weave in our lifetimes, we can understand the psychological tendencies our past has created and prevent them from hijacking our emotions. All of us grew up in less-than-ideal families and social environments, since they were populated by flawed humans, and in these environments learned some ways to emotionally cope and respond before our rational or moral capabilities were fully developed. To identify these scenarios, and the default responses we learned in our formative years, enables us to recognize similar people and circumstances in our lives and proactively engage our higher moral and rational dimensions to prevent us from responding as we did in the past.

Many of you are aware of Professor Daniel Simons' experiment where volunteers were instructed to watch a video and count the number of times a basketball is passed among several people. When asked at the end if they saw anything unusual in the video, the answer was almost universally "no." This, in spite of the fact that a man dressed as a gorilla walked slowly right through the center of the group while they were passing the ball around. But it's not only our physical vision that can play major tricks on us. Our psychological perception can become equally distorted based on past experiences, thus giving us flawed instructions on how to perceive and react to current reality.

Emotionally driven responses in our childhood were not only understandable, but sometimes required for us to effectively cope as children with reality. And as part of this process we attached perceptions and associated meanings to our reality, a psychological necessity for us at the time. As adults, however, though our reality has changed, our formative memories have not, nor likely has the meaning (hashtag if you please) we attached to them. So when we find ourselves in scenarios that resemble those of our childhood (or perhaps mirror traumatic adult experiences), we tend to unconsciously attach the same meaning, thus viewing reality through a very limited and distorted lens. This can prompt us to react as we did when young or traumatized, with emotionally driven decisions and behaviors, neglecting the rational and moral reasoning capabilities we now have at our disposal. These capabilities can be hijacked by the inner child that is alive and well in our unconscious limbic system, especially if we enable it.

Some examples from my life and my work with leaders illustrating this phenomenon would include:

- Those who grew up in an environment where conflict produced painful consequences may have their primal flight (avoidance) emotions triggered, and thus avoid the constructive conflict required for any human, team or organization to learn and grow.

- Those who grew up with too few limits and too much freedom may have suffered some painful consequences as a result, and may now react with undue fear and trepidation when given freedom and authority to act.

- One may sabotage their own success...repeatedly...if they grew up in an environment where they were shamed and their worth diminished. One may also be inclined to sabotage their success if they grew up with excessive praise and reward (too many participation trophies), as they will also associate the meaning and hashtags of "unearned" and "undeserving" with recognition and reward. In both cases guilt and shame left unaddressed may prevent them from ever achieving their potential.

For me personally, the conflict-avoidance tendencies learned in my youth caused me to avoid a new executive I reported to, with unpleasant implications that took over a year to play out. There were several similarities between this situation and my childhood that I should have recognized (e.g., controlling authority figure), but did not until after the fact. As is typical when our inner emotional child starts making decisions in an adult reality, I made some irrational decisions, violated the Golden Rule with my behavior, and paid the price with an unnecessarily stressful year. I cover this scenario in more detail later in the book.

In every scenario where our rational and moral dimensions are hijacked by emotions, violations of integrity and the Golden Rule are almost certain to follow. Thus, in addition to all the relationship and career consequences, we add the guilt and stress of violating our moral compass to the mix. To avoid this toxic mix and its painful consequences:

- Beware advice that all emotions are OK, equal, and to be accepted without judgment as this just reinforces to your inner child that it is acceptable for it to remain in its immature comfort zone.

- Instead, help your inner child to grow up by clearly identifying scenarios and the related emotions that tend to hijack your rational and moral capabilities. Work to discover their root causes by asking "why?" repeatedly until you find the scenario in your history most likely to trigger that emotion. Then write a letter, make a phone call, visit a grave and talk to the deceased, or do whatever your heart tells you is required to forgive, let go and move on from your hijacking inner child.

- As you work to determine root causes, learn to discern emotions that you or others might view as negative, but in fact have their "why" rooted in your higher moral dimension. For example, anger as a form of righteous indignation or dissatisfaction with oneself can be a powerful and positive motivating force.[33]

- Consider journaling as a form of therapy, as writing has proven remarkably effective in addressing the areas above. I recommend *Expressive Writing: Words that Heal* by Professor James Pennebaker for your consideration.

• Recognize similar scenarios in the future (in my case conflict with a strong authority figure), and slow down your response by asking yourself a Golden Rule question (e.g., what is best long-term for everyone?) before reacting. This activates your moral compass and gives it the chance to intervene and preclude your inner child from controlling your response. Your inner child will usually oblige, as it's likely already felt enough pain and will welcome some mature adult intervention.

"They could control his entire environment, they could do what they wanted to his body, but Victor Frankl himself was a self-aware being who could look as an observer at his very involvement. His basic identity was intact. He could decide within himself how all of this was going to affect him. Between what happened to him, or the stimulus, and his response to it, was his freedom or power to choose that response."
— **Stephen Covey,**
The Seven Habits of Highly Successful People

The purpose of asking yourself a Golden Rule or similar question (or just thinking the phrase "Golden Rule") in the space between stimulus and response is to interrupt the unconscious thoughts and impulses produced by flawed beliefs, based on past events, that distort current reality. Imagine, for example, a young child who asked a parent to help them with homework and a parent who responded by saying, "Of course, we will work on it together," but then failed repeatedly to keep that promise. When as an adult that person requests help from a peer or boss, and hears similar language in reply, the unconscious belief associated with that promise may lead them to view it as not only unreliable, but as a prelude to failure. Now imagine how unproductive their unconscious response may be (likely distrust leading to withdrawal) by viewing a sincere commitment through a lens distorted by past experience.

Asking a question that disrupts this unconscious belief and thought process redirects you in a way that your higher moral voice will welcome and support, and that opens up the opportunity for further inquiry and learning. It only takes a fraction of a second for your moral compass to consider the long-term consequences in any scenario and give an answer, and the new process becomes your unconscious default approach with a little practice. This disruption and rewiring works even if we don't believe it will because of the universal values within each of us, but we must have the discipline to do it initially until it becomes second nature. There are a number of other disruptive questions that may be helpful to you in similar scenarios that you may explore in the work of Aaron T. Beck, the founder of Cognitive Behavior Therapy.

> *"Most people use their energy attempting to rearrange circumstances that trigger painful emotions. Changing external circumstances will not change your rigid patterns of emotional response. That requires looking at the patterns themselves."*
> — **Gary Zukav**

Never Sent, Never Signed

Given our human weaknesses, there will be moments of course when we need a longer pause and reflection to assess and manage our emotions, as well as an outlet for them so that they are not expressed or redirected unproductively. Lincoln famously wrote numerous "hot" letters that he never sent, and that after reflection he stored away having written "never sent, never signed" on them. The most notable of these letters he wrote to General Meade expressing his strong displeasure that Meade had failed to pursue Lee's army after the Confederate defeat at Gettysburg. It is instructive to read this letter with Lincoln's emotions in the moment fully expressed:

Washington, July 14, 1863.

Major General Meade

I have just seen your despatch to Gen. Halleck, asking to be relieved of your command, because of a supposed censure of mine– I am very – very – grateful to you for the magnificent success you gave the cause of the country at Gettysburg; and I am sorry now to be the author of the slightest pain to you– But I was in such deep distress myself that I could not restrain some expression of it– I had been oppressed nearly ever since the battles at Gettysburg, by what appeared to be evidences that your self, and Gen. Couch, and Gen. Smith, were not seeking a collision with the enemy, but were trying to get him across the river without another battle. What these evidences were, if you please, I hope to tell you at some time, when we shall both feel better. The case, summarily stated is this. You fought and beat the enemy at Gettysburg; and, of course, to say the least, his loss was as great as yours– He retreated; and you did not; as it seemed to me, pressingly pursue him; but a flood in the river detained him, till, by slow degrees, you were again upon him. You had at least twenty thousand veteran troops directly with you, and as many more raw ones within supporting distance, all in addition to those who fought with you at Gettysburg; while it was not possible that he had received a single recruit; and yet you stood and let the flood run down, bridges be built, and the enemy move away at his leisure, without attacking him. And Couch and Smith! The latter left Carlisle in time, upon all ordinary calculation, to have aided you in the last battle at Gettysburg; but he did not arrive– More At the end of more than ten days, I believe twelve, under constant urging, he reached Hagerstown from Carlisle, which is not an inch over fifty-five miles, if so much. And Couch's movement was very little different–

Again, my dear general, I do not believe you appreciate the magnitude of the misfortune involved in Lee's escape– He was within your easy grasp, and to have closed upon him would, in connection with our other late successes, have ended the war— As it is, the war will be prolonged indefinitely. If you could not safely attack Lee last Monday, how can you possibly do so South of the river, when you can take with you very few more then two thirds of the force you then had in hand? It would be unreasonable to expect, and I do not expect you can now effect much. Your golden opportunity is gone, and I am distressed immeasurably because of it—

I beg you will not consider this a prosecution, or persecution of yourself— As you had learned that I was dissatisfied, I have thought it best to kindly tell you why.[34]

It is very revealing that Lincoln begins this letter with an expression of gratitude, along with an apology, and then spends the bulk of the letter on the details of the incident before briefly mentioning how distressed he was at the end. Further, he explains that he is writing only because Meade has already been informed of his displeasure. One could reasonably question whether this begins to qualify as a "hot" letter with unrestrained and unproductive emotional release, or whether it reflects an appropriate level of righteous indignation, as well as an important learning opportunity for Meade to more aggressively pursue the higher good of ending the war quickly and preserving the Union.

That question I will leave for you to decide, but the letter certainly shows the great self-control Lincoln had developed over the years relative to his emotions. This emotional intelligence, as it is characterized today, is more correctly the strengthening of our higher moral dimension so that it interrupts any unhealthy emotional impulses by sending the cautionary warning signals that we have all felt at times to slow down and reconsider. Such moral growth is so impressive in Lincoln's case because in earlier years he had been quite public and unrestrained in his emotional expression, even to the point of biting personal attacks and sarcasm. The writing of an unsent letter can for us, as it did for Lincoln, provide time for further reflection on what, if any, communication should occur, as well as serve as a valuable mechanism to assess whether our thoughts are being driven from higher or lower moral ground.

The best way to escape the darkness has always been to shine a light.

As credible research progresses, the more we learn that we can be the masters of our emotions like Lincoln, and not the victims of some mysterious primal processes controlled by our amygdala. It was upon the research of Professor Joseph LeDoux, one of the most prominent figures in neuroscience, that Daniel Goleman coined the now popular term "amygdala hijack," referring to how quickly and powerfully our primal emotions can override our rational mind. Yet LeDoux's more recent research found that emotions rely on "higher-order" brain states within our cortical (conscious) brain, rather than being controlled by subcortical (nonconscious) brain circuits within our amygdala,[35] with further recent research confirming his findings.[36] This research is so compelling that Goleman, to his credit, has advocated retiring the term that he coined.[37] Some of us are not surprised by any research showing that our brains are more complex and integrated than previously thought, nor by any findings that our higher-order conscious processes have more input and influence over our unconscious processes than previously recognized. All this is good news, of course, to anyone hoping to create the emotional health and resilience required to lead others effectively.

CHAPTER 4

Concluding Thoughts on our Soular System, Human Nature and Neuroscience

"The principal and proper work of history being to instruct, and enable men by the knowledge of actions past to bear themselves prudently in the present and providently in the future."
— Thomas Hobbes

The collapse of the Dee bridge in Chester, England in 1847 killed five train passengers and resulted in one of the first inquiries into the importance of structural integrity, and how the lack of it can produce catastrophic failure. The major design flaw was that the wrought iron did not reinforce the cast iron, resulting in the gradual weakening of the structure after repeated stress. Humans are fortunate to have been designed to have structural integrity, i.e. for their moral, rational and emotional dimensions to naturally reinforce each other to produce exceptional moral clarity, effective decisions and emotional resilience. When these three dimensions are not properly aligned and integrated under the leadership of our moral dimension, however, we become more internally fragmented, stressed, weaker, and more prone to failure with each new challenge.

And of course the damage goes beyond our psychological and physical health. Others who depend on us suffer harm when we crack under pressure and fail to provide the trustworthy integrity and support they need. Practically all of us face numerous such challenges with significant and enduring consequences to ourselves and others. Those of us who have lived for a few decades know that in almost every life there is an oncoming train with a heavier load than expected, and that most of the time we never see it coming. For us to meet and overcome these challenges, it is imperative that we know the status of our psychological structural integrity and alignment, and since we are blessed to have an organic system, understand how to continually strengthen it rather than facilitate its constant erosion.

It should be no surprise that the human brain, containing on average about 85 billion neurons, with perhaps over 800 trillion possible neural connections (synapses), is proving an almost infinitely complex and daunting challenge relative to understanding this integration. Joshua Greene (Harvard), as noted before, has researched and written extensively on the complexity of this integrated system.[38] Dr. Antonio Damasio,[39] noted author and Professor of Psychology, Philosophy and Neurology at USC describes the brain as a supersystem of systems in his attempts to mitigate the typical reductionist approach to neuroscience. This complex structural integration is far from being fully understood by neuroscientists, who have been generally limited to imaging techniques that penetrate only a few millimeters into the brain, and that measure blood flow rather than the deep cellular-level activities of neurons.[40]

According to Tal Yarkoni, who studies neuroscience research methods at the University of Texas, current imaging limitations mean that "...it's like flying over a city and seeing where the lights are on. If you're in an airplane, you might look out the window and identify a patch of land as a residential area. But it's impossible to know what people are doing in their homes."[41] To circumvent this limitation researchers at the McGovern Institute for Brain Research (MIT) are developing MRI-based calcium sensors that may help to identify deeper cellular-level activity of small clusters of neurons that are involved in specific behaviors or actions.[42] Because this method directly measures signaling within cells, it may offer much more precise information about the location and timing of neuron activity than the traditional functional MRI (fMRI).

There are, of course, other promising developments and much good that has been accomplished in healthcare and other disciplines from current research. But to what degree neuroscience research will offer invaluable insights into how we form beliefs, think, choose and feel emotions remains an open question. Certainly for many of us who believe that we have an eternal, spiritual soul, science will forever fall short of any goal to empirically validate or investigate areas like consciousness or our moral conscience. And no matter our beliefs, most of us believe and wish to certainly be more than just our brain, no matter how much insight science provides.

But despite the limitations and gaps within current research there has been no shortage of hyperbole and outright scientific bunk shared in the race to sound smarter. Among the leading examples are mirror neurons, now widely recognized as the "most hyped concept in neuroscience," with absolutely no basis in research for all the hype.[43] Yet, you will find an incredible variety of articles and speeches explaining how they give us new and profound insights into human empathy, social interaction, emotional intelligence, the formation of cultures and even autism. Theoretically they prompt and even make us feel and respond in kind to the actions and emotions of others (often described as copycat neurons).

All of this based on research just over 20 years old on the macaque monkey, no less. A prominent neuroscientist (Ramachandran) began the hype when he wrote in 2000 that mirror neurons would do for psychology what DNA did for biology. However, subsequent research has not only failed to validate any of his hopeful assumptions, but essentially undermine them, including finding compensating "anti-mirror" neurons in humans. Why so many would be eager to assume that the brain of a monkey, so vastly different from the human brain in scale, structure and complexity, would provide profound and definitive answers to the mysteries of human behavior is a question worth contemplating.[44]

Another fine example, the insular cortex, was not long ago all the rage including a feature in the New York Times, but has now become passé after learning that it lights up in about a third of all fMRI studies no matter what people are asked to do. Many other examples of neuro-hype abound, more than a few of them presumed to provide shortcuts to leadership and relationship effectiveness or rationalizations for human behavior.[45] I would thus encourage a healthy skepticism toward any work or thought that reflects a micro-focus on isolated parts of our complex psychological system, with corresponding hyperbolic statements about their influence or impact. To those of you interested in more along this line of thought, I recommend *Brainwashed, the Seductive Appeal of Mindless Neuroscience,* a finalist for the LA Times Book Prize, which describes how pseudo neuroscience has merged with many other disciplines and has begun to replace personal responsibility as the mechanism of choice to explain unproductive and even criminal behavior.[46]

Are we not better served by focusing on well-established research and our knowledge of thousands of years of human nature to help us better understand and create a well-aligned internal psychological system? It is common knowledge now that research into neuroplasticity has confirmed our ability to make significant progress toward a healthier soular system at any age, no matter how far removed we may be from our ideal state. Just a small change today can disrupt old synaptic patterns enough to make another change easier tomorrow. Since what fires together wires together, it is equally true that our brain adapts to any violations of our moral compass and integrity to make more egregious violations easier, and thus more likely, in the future. The reduced signaling and sensitivity of our amygdala in response to dishonesty has now validated that the "slippery slope" not only exists, but that it is a powerful mechanism we cannot afford to neglect.[47] That same mechanism, of course, can work to our advantage to increase our moral sensitivity, and related leadership influence, as we learn how to align our soular system for greater moral clarity and courage.

It is worthwhile to ask why so much time and energy has been devoted to neuro-hype beyond the limits of credible research. Are we in search of some convenient explanation for human behavior that further removes it from our personal responsibility? That would indeed be consistent with human nature over thousands of years of recorded history. Or do we become so enamored with our latest theoretical construct or presentation theme that cognitive bias blinds us to science? A paper in *Perspectives in Psychological Science* found an epidemic of "puzzlingly high" correlations in neuroscience research and concluded that it is "quite possible that a considerable number of relationships reported in this literature are entirely illusory."[48] Scientific researchers are not immune to confirmation bias, another element of human nature with a long and consistent history.

Of course it is convenient to believe that we may be hard-wired for certain behaviors, or that someone else can "trigger" an emotional response beyond our control, but at what price? When we fail to accept 100% of the responsibility for our behavior, we also give up our response-ability, i.e. our ability to respond differently in the future and improve our life and leadership results. We slowly become powerless victims of synaptic processes, our history or circumstances, or others who have triggered or wronged us...there is never a shortage of blame options from which to choose. And those choices may indeed comfort us, for a little while, until the life consequences of our rationalizations start to catch up with us.

A better path is to pay attention to our thoughts and emotions with the goal of proactively training and wiring them to "fire" in a positive direction until this process is uncon-scious. While neuroscience research is constantly evolving, and far from providing us a definitive understanding of such a complex system, human nature and the moral behavior that influences others has remained remarkably consistent throughout human history. Thus, with conscious focus and practice we can soon develop unconscious habits that increase our leadership influence far beyond our line of sight and even our lifetime. That process we begin to explore now, beginning with the implications of an unaligned and dis-integrating internal soular system.

Reflection & Action

Make a list of key personal and professional decisions you have made over your life, in chronological order, especially those that were challenging to make. After each decision reflect on and capture in as few words as possible why you made that decision.

Write your initial impression first and then keep asking "why?" until you get to a clear root cause statement that captures the ultimate value (priority) that primarily influenced that decision honestly and clearly. Determine whether that root cause driver of your decision was produced primarily from your short-term emotional, rational calculating, or higher moral dimension.

Note the trend over a significant number of years and reflect on which of the three voices you have exercised and strengthened most over time.

This begins the process of bringing our unconscious psychological processes and values into a state of greater consciousness, which gives us the higher perspective and insight to begin changing them. It also begins to awaken, exercise and strengthen our higher moral voice.

PART 2

THE COST OF A DISINTEGRATING SOULAR SYSTEM

CHAPTER 5

The Self-Perpetuating Cycle of Psychological Disintegration

"If only people could realize what an enrichment it is to find one's own guilt, what a sense of honour and spiritual dignity!"
— Carl Jung, *CW 10, Para 416*

"Look not for any greater harm than this: destroying the trustworthy, self-respecting, well-behaved man within you."
— Epictetus

Guilt

Guilt used to have a decent reputation. It was regarded as a signal that we had done something to violate our moral compass that needed correcting. Certainly other unproductive kinds of guilt, often introduced from external sources, were recognized, but guilt was generally understood to be an important sign of a healthy soular system, and a signal that needed

95

to be acted upon immediately. However, as a postmodern ethic emerged, guilt began to carry an increasingly negative connotation. It was something that weighed you down and held you back, and a guilt trip was a dead end to be avoided at all costs. Now popular psychology and coaching on how to rid yourself of any guilt abounds, as if our moral dimension would allow us to remove one of its vital components.

Cycle of Disintegration from Guilt to Shame

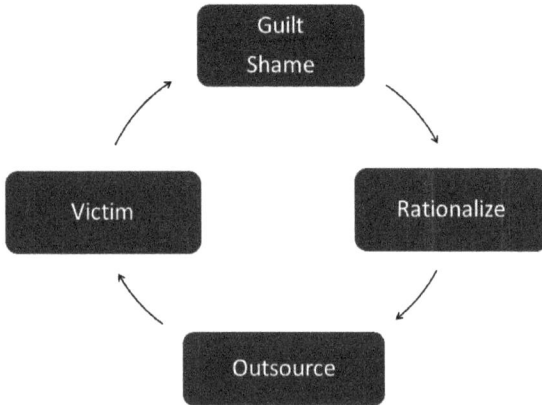

```
        ┌──────────┐
        │  Guilt   │
        │  Shame   │
        └──────────┘
   ↗                    ↘
┌──────────┐        ┌──────────┐
│  Victim  │        │Rationalize│
└──────────┘        └──────────┘
   ↖                    ↙
        ┌──────────┐
        │ Outsource│
        └──────────┘
```

But our moral dimension will not allow us to avoid guilt, as it serves as our critical early warning signal to alert us when we have done something wrong and need to make right whatever we have done to violate the Golden Rule or our integrity. This early warning system is so sensitive, if we keep it in good working order, that we can feel ourselves getting psychologically weaker and dis-integrating within at the first thought of lying or doing something we know to be wrong. If we then respond to this tinge of guilt before we act, and redirect our thoughts toward what we know is right, we conversely can feel ourselves becoming internally stronger and more integrated, because in fact we are.

This early warning system even activates when those who would influence us negatively come around, like radar detecting approaching enemy aircraft. It is indeed a marvelous blessing to have this early warning system as part of our moral dimension, as ethical experiments and research have found that guilt-proneness (the proactive guilt that prevents wrongdoing as described above) is more predictive of trust-worthy behavior than other traits we normally associate with trust.[49] Thus recognizing and responding to this early warning guilt is an absolute prerequisite to building the trust required for effective leadership.

> *Do we embrace guilt as our friend, or are we trying to suppress and avoid its proactive messages?*

Lincoln illustrated this correlation between responding proactively to guilt and future trustworthiness, even early in his youth. Stories from those who knew him abound about how he rescued turtles, cats, dogs, birds and even a pig from cruelty or peril. Mary Vineyard told Lincoln's law partner William Herndon the story of Lincoln passing by a pig mired in a bog without stopping to render aid because he was so well dressed. A bit after passing, however, he began to feel guilty for not rescuing the hog, so he promptly turned back and went to work saving it. Even at the age of ten he intervened after seeing a group of boys placing hot coals on the backs of turtles, and shortly thereafter wrote an essay on the treatment of animals and presented it publicly at school.

I suspect some of you may be wondering why I chose such insignificant stories, about animals rather than humans no less, to try and illustrate such an important point. Precisely because these are the everyday, common moments in our lives that we deem of little to no consequence. And yet each time we feel even a slight tinge of guilt in such an "insignificant" moment, and choose to ignore and suppress it, we ensure that the guilt signals we feel in the future will be weaker, no matter how small or big the moment. The great leaders I've been blessed to know have all spoken about how we can judge character by how people treat children and animals, or those powerless to provide any meaningful consequences to our behavior. When we start to appreciate that how we respond to a slight nudge from our conscience in these moments is absolutely predictive of our future trustworthiness and influence in matters both great and small, we begin to understand why so many leaders fall short of the Lincoln standard.

Clayton Christensen, the beloved Harvard Professor who was named the top management thinker in the world, talked often about the life-changing power of one such "small" decision he made while a student at Oxford and a member of the varsity basketball team. The team had made it through the equivalent of the NCAA tournament and was scheduled to play in the championship game on a Sunday. Of course

Christensen desperately wanted to play, but having made a commitment to God to never play on Sundays, every time he tried to rationalize the choice to play he felt a touch of guilt. So he decided to respect his divinely embedded higher voice and told the coach that he would not be playing. The coach was incredulous and his teammates tried to talk him into playing and violating his rule just this one time. But Clayton Christensen refused to play (the team won anyway), standing alone on principle as did Lincoln with his perspective on the treatment of animals.

In the years afterward Christensen often spoke of the profound positive influence that one decision to respect and respond proactively to his guilt had on the rest of his life:

"In many ways that was a small decision—involving one of several thousand Sundays in my life. In theory, surely I could have crossed over the line just that one time and then not done it again. But looking back on it, resisting the temptation whose logic was "In this extenuating circumstance, just this once, it's OK" has proven to be one of the most important decisions of my life. Why? My life has been one unending stream of extenuating circumstances. Had I crossed the line that one time, I would have done it over and over in the years that followed.

The lesson I learned from this is that it's easier to hold to your principles 100% of the time than it is to hold to them 98% of the time. If you give in to "just this once," based on a marginal cost analysis, as some of my former classmates have done, you'll regret where you end up. You've got to define for yourself what you stand for and draw the line in a safe place."[50]

If you are not familiar with the impact of his ideas and the profound influence Christensen had upon so many, it will not take you long to validate both. His choice to respect and respond to guilt proactively, in a scenario that most would deem inconsequential, had a lifetime impact on the health of his soular system. No wonder, like Lincoln, he was known as such a kind and charitable man, and no wonder he had the tremendous cerebral free space to form and refine such innovative and powerful ideas.

It's not hard to validate the lifelong positive or crippling effect from how we respond to guilt, because we can actually feel ourselves getting stronger or weaker by just thinking about our options. We can feel the peace and strength when thinking of a higher moral option, as well as the stress, weakness and need for endless justification created by thinking of options driven by our rational ("marginal cost analysis") or emotional voice. Pausing and paying attention to these signals before choosing or speaking, no matter how small or great the moment appears, makes all the difference in our character and leadership impact over our lifetime.

Rationalize

If we disregard the proactive physiological and psychological signals that guilt produces, and turn our thoughts into actions that violate the Golden Rule or our integrity, then our conscience immediately begins to trouble us with even more guilt, along with an urgent demand for an explanation. The purpose of this double whammy is to prompt us to immediately correct our path, apologize and do whatever possible to undo any harm we may have caused. However, too often we choose to begin an internal dialogue with our moral compass: one intent on building a defense for ourselves, in spite of the fact that we have firsthand knowledge of our guilt. How we can delude ourselves to continue down this path with any expectation of a happy ending is one of the great mysteries of the human condition, but a universal one it seems.

This path of course requires that we begin to create and embellish a false narrative, distort some facts and disregard others, all the while searching for witnesses who will corroborate our version of reality and exonerate us from any wrongdoing. These mental gyrations continue, even as we sleep, in desperate attempts to assuage our guilt and provide an acceptable explanation to our conscience, who keeps us on constant trial until we either provide such an explanation or plead guilty. Since, in fact, we are guilty of doing what we knew to be wrong at the time, we are set upon an untenable course of internal stress and dis-ease that either brings us to our senses, or further perpetuates a cycle that only becomes increasingly darker and harder to escape.

Outsource

Persistence along this path, in spite of its psychic energy-consuming cost and damage, eventually seems to provide a resolution, as usually there is someone else in the scenario who has hurt us or done us wrong in some way. If not, time will usually allow us to distort the facts and embellish our false narrative so much that we can convince ourselves of their guilt, even if they are innocent. Thus we can now blame someone else for our sins, conveniently turning our wrong actions into a justifiable and even normal human response.

The problem is that we have compounded our guilt by lying even more egregiously to ourselves, as well as to anyone who will listen to our tragic story. Compounded our guilt because our moral dimension has now indicted us on many more counts of moral corruption and lying. By now, however, we have likely began to suppress that guilt by pushing it into our unconscious, because unless we are losing our sanity through this process (literally), we cannot consciously tolerate such a doubling-down on our initial wrongdoing and the person we are becoming.

To keep our guilt mostly unconscious and preserve our sanity, however, requires a nearly fulltime investment in continually retelling and reinforcing the false narrative that we have now constructed, and likely even convinced ourselves at a conscious level to be true. More than a few of you have sat down by a complete stranger on an airplane, or in a coffee shop, and found yourself soon listening to a story of how wronged they were by their ex-spouse or an evil boss, and how they were left no choice but to ultimately do something completely out of character for them, but at the same time absolutely necessary under the circumstances. With the understanding that not that a single one of us has ever been that person…of course not!

The toxic emotions that we stir up and fuel ever stronger in this process, anger, bitterness, resentment etc., leave no room for happiness or inner peace and create neural storms that cripple whatever critical-thinking or creative capabilities we may have previously enjoyed. Our brains respond as you would expect people in a meeting to react if loud and distracting noises were coming into the meeting room through an open door.[51] Someone would get up and close the door. Synaptic pathways that integrate our moral, rational and emotional systems thus begin to close from the noise and stress created by these neural storms, which has frightening enough implications for personal relationships and decision-making capabilities, but is even more crippling for a leader. A Yale study[52] found that the long-term effects of such stress cause our brain not only to shrink, but as described by neuroscientist David Eaglemen, also causes stress hormones to eat away at brain tissue, literally chewing miniature holes in our brains.[53]

We have now begun to isolate, rather than integrate, our moral, rational and emotional dimensions, as well as strengthen either our rational or emotional voice to dominate and lead our inner soular system. These increasingly one-dimensional leaders are not hard to recognize, but tragically, for them this has become an unconscious process that distorts reality and cripples their ability to think critically, make effective decisions or build healthy relationships. It is not a long journey to the point where most of what they think and do is in service to the mission of perpetuating the delusional reality they have constructed, and to prevent any sliver of truth from penetrating this fantasy world, since unconsciously they know how fragile its construction is. Their soular system, no longer held together by the pull of a strong moral compass at the center, is slowly expanding and dying, becoming increasingly influenced by and reactive to its environment, rather than a proactive system determining its own future direction and destiny.

Victim

The end state of this tragic self-inflicted damage is the ultimate delusion that we are a powerless victim, the antithesis of leadership, because we have chosen to abdicate the responsibility for our own choices and behavior, and thus our future, to others. Such a person cannot lead anyone forward because they remain forever trapped in their own past, spending most of their life's energy in futile attempts to bolster the false narratives they have created. Completely futile attempts because our moral conscience does not buy fiction, but only the truth.

How completely devastating this delusional victim state can become is illustrated by the words and actions of many public leaders who have crashed and burned right before our eyes. Among the more recent ones is Carlos Ghosn, who was arrested in Japan for underreporting his pay as CEO of Nissan, as well as for using company assets for personal purposes. I chose this example because Ghosn was not arrested nor accused of what we would view as the more egregious ethical violations of Elizabeth Holmes et al., but of what many would consider a smaller and less significant issue, likely in response to the public concern over CEO pay in France and Japan.[54] In other words, behavior that could easily be justified, which is precisely how Ghosn responded.

In fact, after fleeing Japan by hiding himself in a box for musical equipment on a private jet, Ghosn later said in a Beirut news conference that he had "no other choice" but to flee Japan and his upcoming trial. This is a striking statement for such an intelligent person to make, as he obviously had multiple choices he could have made, and yet he made this statement with absolute sincerity knowing that it was being broadcast around the world. This should be a shocking example of just how delusional we can become over time, to the point of consciously believing and publicly stating something completely detached from reality.

It is equally instructive to learn that Ghosn did not suddenly arrive at this delusional victim state. He had been paying his sister large sums of money for consulting services that were never provided, as well as providing her a luxury condo with company funds.[55] Given the large breadth of power he was granted as CEO of the world's largest automobile consortium, over time he made and rationalized a number of "small" moral violations that ultimately brought him to this tragic end. As cited by the research previously mentioned, each one of these violations, no matter how insignificantly we or others may view it, reduces the warning signals of guilt produced by our amygdala to make future violations not only easier, but also ensuring that our moral voice becomes weaker and quieter with each transgression. No wonder Lincoln viewed even the telling of an insincere truth as lying, given this very slippery moral slope, and hopefully a wakeup call to us for saying such "harmless" expressions as "Just tell them that I'm not in."

Though few leaders arrive at such public and dramatic ends, no less tragic is the self-inflicted damage many suffer from traveling this path of self-delusion. Fairly early in my consulting career I was standing on a Cape Cod beach with my mentor, talking with a senior leader at a major company about the challenges he was facing with a recent acquisition. Although years ago, I clearly remember the strained emotion in his voice as he said, speaking about the future job security of some of the acquired employees, "I feel so badly that I have to lie to them." Obviously, he had been given precise instructions on the M&A messaging he was to give, even though he knew that it was not going to be true for all employees. Yet, here is another leader who had become so delusional as to convince himself that he had to lie, when clearly there were multiple other options available to him. But tragically, he was becoming powerless to chart his own future growth and influence as a moral leader by embedding within his unconsciousness another cycle of endless guilt, rationalization, outsourcing blame and victimization that would greatly damage him personally and professionally.

The single most powerful act most of us can do to strengthen our moral dimension, increase the health of our psychological soular system, and avoid this tragic state is to identify the false narratives we have constructed over the years in the futile attempts to justify our wrong behavior, and then do whatever possible to take responsibility for and repair the damage. Beyond that, we can increase our future emotional and psychological health by recognizing and proactively responding to guilt so we can prevent thoughts from turning into communication or behavior that violates the Golden Rule or our integrity. There is no question where what we may perceive as "small" moral violations are going to lead, as natural law dictates that we will eventually reap what we sow. The problem for many is that the time between sowing and fully reaping the harvest in natural law is so long that they cannot see the ultimate destiny they are choosing. Nothing distinguishes a great leader like Lincoln more than the ability to see the ultimate harvest when a small seed is being planted.

To consciously recognize and unravel these false narratives, however, requires some deep reflection and painful work initially for most of us. Solzhenitsyn wrote that it was only after years of lying on the rotting prison straw that he began to recognize these narratives in his past and recognize the true meaning of moral and good behavior. In the same passage he writes that "In my most evil moments I was convinced that I was doing good, and I was well supplied with systematic arguments."[56] The path that he took to the moral high ground, which produced such leadership influence that the New York Times described him as the man who destroyed an evil empire from the inside of a prison cell,[57] is one that may be initially as uncomfortable as lying on the rotting straw in a gulag. But the transcendent influence, power and inner peace of such a journey, as illustrated by Lincoln, makes it the most valuable investment, with the highest return, that we will ever make. Because as we continually exercise and strengthen our moral dimension and its early warning system, we become more unconsciously competent in moral thoughts and behavior, avoiding these self-destructive cycles and the suffering that so many choose to endure.

> *Doing what is right does not require arguments or rationalizations. The right thing to do is almost always self-evident.*

Shame

In Carlo Collodi's "The Adventures of Pinocchio" the lad Pinocchio tells a lie about losing his coins, but what seems a reasonable and harmless one given that earlier he had been cheated. As his lies compound to cover his original lie, he finally asks the fairy how she knows he is lying. To which the fairy responds, "Lies, my dear boy, are found out immediately, because they are of two sorts. There are lies that have short legs, and lies that have long noses. Your lie, as it happens, is one of those that have a long nose."

Lies with short legs are obvious because the truth is so self-evident. Lies with long noses are obvious to most everyone but the liar, who is naïve enough to believe they can keep lying and get away with it. From Aesop to Aristotle to Machiavelli, great thinkers have recognized there are no harmless or white lies because of the damaging consequences to the person speaking the lie. In Pinocchio's case his nose, or guilt, grew so large that that it turned into shame for the person he had become. At that point his shame was such a burden and constraint on him that his nose wouldn't fit through the door. Guilt that is not acted upon to correct our wrongs eventually turns into such a prison of shame that we turn into a small and miserable bundle, all tangled up within ourselves, unable to escape from our self-constructed prison any more than a lie can outrun the truth.

The moral to Pinocchio's story is simply that only the truth will set us free, while lying to ourselves to justify our wrongs, or lying to others, ultimately enslaves us, no matter how oblivious we may be to the incremental but insidious construction of our self-imposed imprisonment. Honoring and speaking the truth, about ourselves especially, is the first step to growing up and having the chance to be an authentic and moral human, which is an absolute prerequisite to leadership influence.

CHAPTER 6

Collusion Circles and Triangles

Collusion With Those Who are Innocent

I first began to recognize the deeper implications of our lack of integrity on others and organizational culture when I first came across the work of Chris Argyris, the Harvard professor who was a pioneer in the areas of organizational learning and development. Argyris described how we can begin to appreciate the effect of our lack of full integrity and transparency on others by simply using two columns. A left-hand column in which we write what we actually thought while in conversation with another person, then a right-hand column in which we write what we actually said. Looking at the discrepancies between the two, it is easy to see how others not only develop incomplete and distorted perceptions of reality, but act upon that perception in ways that damage others and the organization.[58]

I still clearly remember a compelling example of my failure in this area when I was just a youngster in my late 20's working as a frontline manager in the FedEx Memphis Hub. I was asked by my Senior Manager at the time if I would take responsibility for the full mini-sort that occurred nightly at the end of the main sort. The mini-sort involved processing thousands of packages or documents that had been missorted during the night and needed to be directed to the correct flight to reach their intended destination. I was at the time responsible for half the employees doing this work, while the manager responsible for the other half had left their position. This was an intense and high-pressure process that needed to be completed within about half an hour and meant that I would now be responsible for the supervision of about sixty employees rather than thirty.

Of course I voiced my willingness to assume this responsibility, in spite of the fact that it was during the peak Christmas shipping season, and that I would be moving immediately after Christmas to begin a new field position in Chicago. After all, how could my last major work decision in Memphis be to express reluctance to accept additional responsibility? Who knows when that might come back to haunt me, so my rational dimension led me to enthusiastically accept the assignment in spite of my inner doubts about how I would handle such responsibility while preparing to move and during the most challenging time of the year.

The Self-Perpetuating Cycle of Collusion

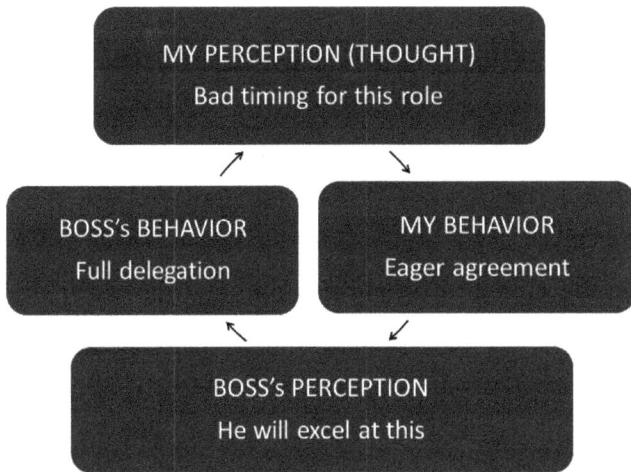

As fate would have it a major change in aircraft gate assignments was to be implemented on the first work night after my last day in Memphis. My boss stressed the importance of these changes, and I met with the team leaders before I left to go over the changes and stress their importance. I found out later in a note from my boss that something went wrong that night, resulting in some packages from the mini-sort being routed to the wrong aircraft gates, and then being held in Memphis and later expedited on other airlines…not only missing their delivery commitments but incurring great additional costs as well. Never in my career, before or since, have I been part of any error remotely approaching this significance.

For years afterward this bothered me, and I continued to feel frustration over the fact that an experienced Senior Manager had asked me, during peak season, while preparing for a move, and just a youngster to boot, to assume such responsibility. I have no idea what went wrong that night, but I blamed my boss for giving me that assignment when he could have asked someone more experienced to help, as well as more closely checked that night to make sure the changes had been understood and implemented. But eventually I came around to asking why, if I bore no fault in the matter, was it still a source of ongoing frustration and resentment? It was years later when I recognized that my inner dis-ease over this scenario was due to the fact that I had not been honest when first offered the opportunity, something my unconscious had been prompting me to recognize and learn from for all those years.

It would be frightening to be able to calculate the amount of psychic energy consumed and the stress created by the cycle of rationalization, the outsourcing of blame and the victim status that I created and perpetuated over the years. To recognize and learn from these unconscious cycles, and their extended harmful consequences, is a major step toward understanding the price we pay for "small" violations of integrity. It's should not be hard to imagine the enormous price to ourselves and other innocent victims should we practice this integrity gap as a matter of habit.

Collusion With Willing Partners

Earlier in this book I wrote about how I reacted to a new VP, who had a very different leadership style from me, and whom I had been told by a credible source was "out to get me." My choice at the time, however, seemed to me entirely rational while avoiding any short-term emotional distress. I just avoided them, rather than aligning my words with what I was actually thinking and confronting them in an attempt to constructively and proactively resolve the situation. As I outlined earlier, my failure to take a longer-term Golden Rule view of my behavior resulted in an unnecessarily stressful year for me and lost opportunity costs for those around me because of my self-protective reaction. As illustrated, my reaction accomplished nothing beyond incentivizing and increasing the behavior of my new boss, which was by all indications on a lower moral plane also, intent on removing someone who did not align with their ideal leadership style.

The Self-Perpetuating Cycle of Collusion

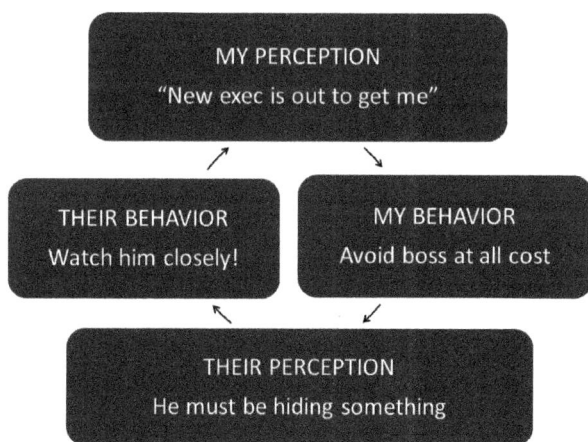

MY PERCEPTION
"New exec is out to get me"

THEIR BEHAVIOR
Watch him closely!

MY BEHAVIOR
Avoid boss at all cost

THEIR PERCEPTION
He must be hiding something

I learned the depth of their intent, along with the futility and unintended consequences of my behavior, when I was given my first performance review by this new boss. Having received the highest possible rating and an award from my prior VP, I was certainly prepared for a totally different experience, however, I vastly underestimated what that difference would be. Since there was no way to "get me" in any operational performance areas, I was given an unsatisfactory rating in two leadership areas:

- Integrity: The boss informed me that I had in essence lied on an expense report from months before when I had driven to a staff meeting. I had recorded slightly more mileage for the trip than their direct route calculation, and thus had filed an expense report with a few more dollars due me than the boss deemed appropriate. As this trip took me through Dallas I had, as was my custom, driven around the city rather than take the direct route through, to avoid traffic and the hassle. I was so taken aback that I failed to inquire why a lack of integrity would be assumed without prior conversation, or ask who would be foolish enough to add a few miles to get a few dollars more at my salary, or why someone trusted with so many people and millions of dollars was not allowed to determine their own driving route within reason.

- Decision-making: I had taken a half-day from the office to take our staff person responsible for quality programs with me to look for a good location to conduct an outdoor-based leadership simulation for our senior management staff. I so informed the office and spent much of the driving time in discussion with our head of quality on how to ensure our new initiatives would be successful, which was equally my intent for that half-day excursion. Once again, as a total surprise when my review was given, I was rated unsatisfactory in decision-making for "wasting" half a day. I was too shocked at this point to respond or rebut effectively. Two things were clear, the "out to get me" warning was not only true, but someone in the office was giving ammunition to the new boss on anything that might not fit her ideal leadership model and thus could be used to lower my rating, in spite of our continued strong operational performance.

As you can easily detect, this was a quite shocking and unpleasant experience, but it only helped me rationalize and deepen my self-protective behavior until I was able to find a role in another region. In the meantime I doubled down on my efforts to seek out and communicate primarily with those whom I thought to be sympathetic to my plight, as well as support my rationalizations for the lack of moral integrity and courage to directly address this behavior. "Fortunately" for me, there was no shortage of people who did not care for my boss along with other prior casualties who were more than happy to vent their feelings. This dynamic produces triangulation involving multiple people where everyone is seeking to validate their perspective or behavior and invalidate anyone with a different or higher perspective that might produce learning and growth. But as my friend and former FedEx colleague Steve Nielsen reminded me, it can be frightening how quickly we become trapped in these cycles, how unconscious we can be of objective reality, and how even whom we involve in our "water cooler" conversations becomes driven by our need to reinforce our lower and distorted perspectives.

Collusion & Triangulation

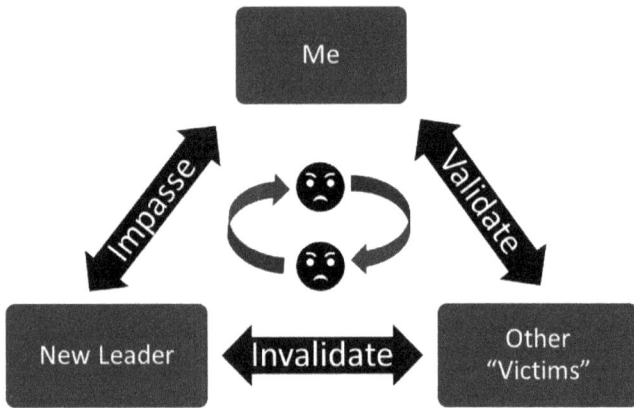

We are so easily drawn into these cycles because of how leaders tend to keep score. Rebecca Chou was the leader of the HR function at a major airline when she was responsible for accelerating my early career success with our leadership programs. She has been successful in numerous executive roles and positively influenced many people during her career because, as she emphasized to me, she measures her success by an internal scorecard rather than by an external one. My performance in the Managing Director role at FedEx, by any external performance metrics, was a clear success. Yet the fact that these external metrics were my primary scorecard was precisely why it took a few years for me to become conscious of the cycle of collusion that I became entangled in.

Had I been evaluating my performance primarily based on an internal scorecard, one that measured the alignment of my decisions and behavior with the highest moral standards, I would have evaluated myself differently and avoided these cycles altogether, or worst case, recognized and corrected them much earlier. To measure our success primarily by this internal scorecard guarantees our continued growth in moral clarity and courage, and thus our future leadership success, since we are continually increasing both the depth and reach of our influence. I could give you no more powerful or practical recommendation than to begin journaling your daily leadership progress as measured by an internal moral scorecard, which for me, has these components:

1. Have I told the truth?

2. Has every word spoken reflected what I sincerely and deeply believed or felt? Has a single word been spoken insincerely to avoid conflict, advance my career, or appease others?

3. Has each decision and action been in the best long-term interest of the most people affected?

Just beginning this process is an empowering and liberating event, as it signals our moral compass to wake up and begin serving in its designed leadership role for our internal soular system. And as we exercise and strengthen our higher moral voice daily, we increasingly recognize and are able to help others avoid these self-perpetuating and destructive cycles. As did Lincoln, we daily increase our ability to perceive the moral implications of each communication and action, and thus begin to elicit the levels of trust and respect earned by very few leaders.

The Ultimate Price

Forty-seven years ago the cargo ship Edmund Fitzgerald sunk during a storm on Lake Superior. All twenty-nine crew were lost just fifteen miles from the safety of Whitefish Bay, and many of you will recall the Gordon Lightfoot hit song that memorialized the crew. Given the Captain's course many experts think the ship would have made those last fifteen miles with a little more depth clearance, as was reported in the National Transportation Board's accident report and analysis.[59] But prior to this trip the shipping company successfully convinced the Coast Guard to eliminate the "insignificant" winter requirements for a slightly lighter load, so their profit would not be reduced during those few months. Those safety regulations had given the ship a few more feet of clearance during the volatile fall and winter weather. The crew talked openly about the increased risk among themselves and their families, and certainly did not like the change, but in fear of their jobs, apparently no one had the courage to voice their concerns openly.

Over four decades later Boeing leaders convinced the FAA to accept "small" changes to the autopilot operation (MCAS) of the new 737 MAX without requiring expensive new simulator training for pilots already certified to fly the 737. Some inside the company quietly shared their concerns with each other. It was not until 348 souls perished in two related crashes, however, that numerous people shared these concerns openly. The House Transportation Committee in its final report described a "culture of concealment" that enabled the company to avoid expensive and time-consuming regulatory oversight from the FAA that would have reduced profit and put Boeing further behind in their effort to compete with Airbus.[60]

Note how ostensibly self-protective mechanisms, whether they be withholding our true thoughts and remaining silent, or behaving in ways to protect our short-term interests, can spread like a virus to consume teams, departments, functions and even a company's culture. I've seen numerous examples of this in my leadership interventions, and in each case the root cause began with an individual leader or a small group of people who seemed oblivious to the fact that we eventually reap what we sow, and who failed to understand that there is no way to predict the final scale or costs to ourselves and others when the seeds of lower moral behavior are planted.

> *"Karma is Undefeated."*
> **– Jeffrey P. McNulty,**
> **author of** *The Ultimate Retail Manual*

It's More Than Business, It's Personal

Many participants in our leadership program have chosen a non-business cycle of collusion as their highest leverage opportunity for growth because they recognized how much it was diminishing their ability to lead effectively. One of these participants, a senior executive in a major company, chose to disclose a cycle that ended with divorce after many years of marriage. In short, during a stressful time at work he began stopping by a local bar to discuss ideas with some fellow employees at the end of the day and relieve some of his stress. His wife confronted him after a couple of days, accusing him of caring more for work than for her. The next day he stayed longer at the bar, reluctant to go home and confront her. As you might expect, the nature of her confrontations escalated and so he began staying even later. Around and around they went, each behaving in a way to prompt the other's lower moral behavior so each of them could continue to justify their own lower behavior. He illustrated their cycle like this:

The Self-Perpetuating Cycle of Collusion

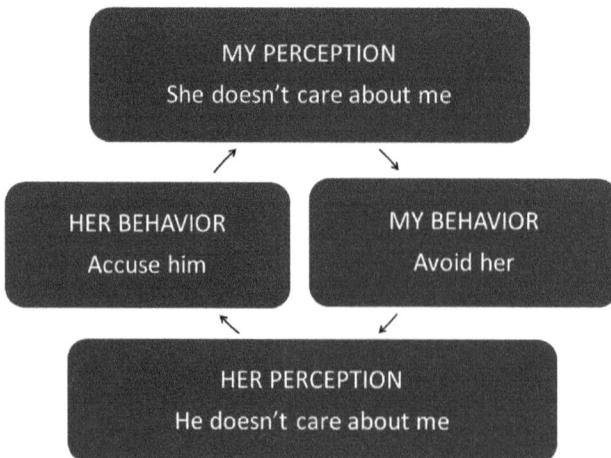

```
              ┌─────────────────────────────┐
              │      MY PERCEPTION           │
              │  She doesn't care about me   │
              └─────────────────────────────┘
                  ↗                    ↘
┌──────────────────────┐      ┌──────────────────────┐
│    HER BEHAVIOR       │      │    MY BEHAVIOR        │
│     Accuse him        │      │      Avoid her        │
└──────────────────────┘      └──────────────────────┘
                  ↖                    ↙
              ┌─────────────────────────────┐
              │      HER PERCEPTION          │
              │  He doesn't care about me    │
              └─────────────────────────────┘
```

What he realized about this cycle that caused him to become so emotional, and to his credit determined to help others through his insights, was:

1. How a challenge that seems confusing and intractable in the moment can be reduced to such simplicity beyond complexity that the root causes and solutions become obvious.

2. That reaching this higher ground where wisdom is available and a resolution possible requires an objective moral perspective, as though standing outside the scenario and viewing it as a disinterested party.

3. That this higher perspective and resolution can never be reached unless one person elevates their perspective and behavior. Both he and his wife refused to do so. Why? Because they both needed the other person to persist in their lower behavior, as the continuation of that lower behavior provided justification for their own emotionally driven reaction. Had either one of them ceased their behavior and elevated it to a higher plane, the law of stimulus and response would have practically guaranteed a positive response from the other and a peaceful resolution. But elevating their behavior would have required admitting that they had been wrong. And both of them preferred to persist in their delusion of being "right" rather than to resolve their conflict.

Thus they continued to strengthen and deepen this cycle over time, outsourcing the blame for their own behavior to each other, each clinging for dear life to the false notion that they were a victim rather than a willing and eager contributor to this toxic cycle. Obviously the toxic emotions and neural storms created within by continually trying to sell a fictional narrative to his moral compass took an enormous toll on this man's ability to lead effectively.

Over the course of human history many lives have been lost due to "insignificant" moral breeches and shortages of courage selfishly justified. From other "small" violations of moral clarity and integrity countless lives, hearts and relationships have been forever damaged in ways that will never be seen or known by the public. Effective leaders have the courage never to make or accept any "small" or "just this once" moral compromises, because they know there is no way to predict the ultimate cost of even the slightest off-course deviation when we allow our rational or emotional voice to lead our soular system.

Most of the balance of this book is focused on how you can achieve the highest level of moral clarity and courage, along with how to leverage its many benefits for yourself and your organization in areas like purpose, strategy, and decision-making. We will also explore how to build a culture on the moral high ground that prevents team and organizational disintegration from these insidious cycles of destruction.

Reflection & Action

Identify any cycles of guilt, rationalization and outsourcing of blame that led you to adopt a victim status. This is best done by reflecting on any bitterness, anger and resentment you still feel (as opposed to legitimate hurt and pain) towards another individual.

In almost every case, you will be able to identify a way in which you violated the Golden Rule or your integrity, and thus your moral compass, in spite of how much wrong the other party did or how they treated you. Do whatever your higher moral voice ask of you to repair past damage, right any wrongs, apologize, ask for forgiveness, etc., whether in writing or in person.

Identify any cycles of collusion you are participating in and take whatever action is required to exit those cycles and challenge those still participating to do likewise.

This will continue the process of bringing unconscious cycles into your conscious mind and will further exercise and strengthen your higher moral voice. To reflect and take corrective action on these cycles is a major step to consciously and proactively recognizing and avoiding them in the future.

Intermission
No Country for Old Men

A store owner in No Country for Old Men unexpectedly
encounters fate in the person of Anton Chigurh in the
famous life or death coin toss scene. The owner manages a
small store and gas station in the middle of nowhere in the
desert of West Texas. He imagines himself isolated from any
ugly twist of fate like the one that shows up in the person of
Chigurh. But none of us is that isolated or protected.

For those of you who haven't read the book or seen the
movie, Anton Chigurh has a twisted moral code that he
follows religiously. If he asks you to call a coin toss, and you
call it right, you live. Call it wrong and your life is over, no
exceptions for Anton.

The store owner is totally unprepared, has no idea what
Chigurh is up to with his coin toss, and tries to avoid calling
the toss by protesting, "But I didn't put nothin' up."

To which Chigurh replies, "Yes, you did. You've been putting it up your whole life, you just didn't know it."

In every life there are moments when fate throws us a curve ball to which we must immediately respond. Decisions we cannot deliberate on, delay or delegate. Often these moments require exceptional moral clarity and courage in order to avoid a lifetime of painful consequences. Spiritual, family and career health, life or death may hang in the balance.

We prepare for these moments our whole life, it just never occurs to some. They fail to recognize that in all their past "insignificant" choices between right and wrong, integrity or duplicity, they have been creating the character that will be revealed in their most trying moments of truth. The character they have built will be the one that shows up, because it's the only one there to answer the call.

Fate will eventually visit us all with an unexpected coin toss and we will have to call it. What have you been putting up your whole life? Are you prepared to make the right call?

PART 3

TAKE AND HOLD THE HIGH GROUND: THE LEADERSHIP ROI

CHAPTER 8

Vision and Strategy: Moral Leaders Take and Hold the High Ground

"A genuine leader is not a searcher for consensus but a molder of consensus."
— Martin Luther King Jr., 1967

Vision

Martin Luther King Jr. illustrated how moral character does much more than just produce the trust, respect and influence required for effective leadership. Standing on higher moral ground also increases our vision. People are now ready to follow, but the question remains, why should they? Where in the world are we going?

Living with moral integrity increases our moral vision, i.e. our ability to see more clearly the gaps between current reality and what is best for our clients, customers and society in the long term. With this insight we can create a higher purpose for our life and a vision for our enterprise that inspires others not only to follow, but fully invest themselves. This clarity of vision enables us to communicate in morally compelling and concrete language, rather than in fuzzy or lofty terms that raise more questions than provide answers. Research informs us that "blurry visions" (e.g. make the world a better place) do not inspire people to follow, even when they trust and respect the leader.[61]

Dr. King's vision still inspires millions to action because he saw the gaps in our society with such moral depth and clarity. In his famous "I have a dream" speech in 1963, after speaking of the promissory note of inalienable rights and equality of all men promised by our founders, he described how America has "defaulted on this note" and instead of honoring this "sacred obligation" has written a bad check which has come back marked "insufficient funds." There is nothing esoteric or lofty about these words. He used concrete and practical analogies that any person could not only relate to, but would find so morally convicting that they would be compelled to act.

Dr. King's dream of the future his vision would create was no less concrete, vivid and inspiring. "I have a dream that one day on the red hills of Georgia the sons of former slaves and sons of former slaveowners will be able to...." Most of us, I suspect, can finish that sentence because the picture it paints is so morally compelling and powerful that it has been seared into our memories. Equally clear and concrete his dream that

132

"my four little children will one day live in a nation where they will be judged not by the color of their skin, but by the content of their character."

The impact of such moral clarity and insight is why I still recall vividly, as if it were yesterday, the first time I heard Fred Smith speak. I was a young manager attending required training at the company's leadership institute. Mr. Smith articulated a clear and compelling vision, based on higher moral principles, of enriching lives and empowering people in every corner of the world, especially in impoverished nations, through the global reach of FedEx. He spoke in concrete language of how the pursuit of that noble vision would change lives and how he was devoted to building a company that also respected and empowered those who would join him in turning that vision into a reality. The golden thread running through this vision was his inherent respect for the dignity and worth of every individual, and his uncompromising devotion to that golden thread has turned his lofty and remarkable dream into reality within my lifetime.

A vision driven by a sincere belief in and devotion to the Golden Rule can be just as powerful for something as ordinary as soap. It is instructive to read of William Lever's construction of Port Sunlight in 1888, a village with model housing, schools and a hospital so his factory workers could enjoy living facilities and amenities beyond the normal mundane wages and standards of the time. This striking investment came only three years after he launched the first branded soap and would certainly be considered a foolhardy risk by many business experts. Yet, as with Fred Smith, he was compelled by his moral principles to maintain the integrity of his vision without compromise, and you can follow that thread from 1847 through to the Unilever of today. While less than 60 of the Fortune 500 from 1955 remain on the list, those leaders whose vision is grounded in higher universal values sustain their enterprises by drawing from the deepest wells of human admiration and loyalty in their customers and employees.

Strategy

The outcome of the battle of Gettysburg in the Civil War was predictable long before the battle ended. Predictable because the Union army held the high ground on three ridges to the south of town due to General John Buford's strategic vision and initiative. While the Confederate army was dispersed over a seven-mile area, the Union's compact position, anchored on several hills, facilitated communication and agile troop deployment. The information flow to Union General Meade from his subordinates was much quicker and more accurate. These contrasting positions and dynamics, as with war in general, hold many lessons applicable to the higher ground of moral leadership as it relates to both vision and strategy.

In life and business, when we occupy the higher ground of moral character and integrity, we have the longer and deeper vision to see the full implications of our decisions and actions much farther down the road, with greater clarity and insight than

others, and are thus able to avoid the unintended consequences and defeats that many suffer. As a result, we have the perspective and wisdom to identify, take and hold without compromise the high ground in formulating and executing a strategy. These extraordinary leadership capabilities elicit the trust and respect required to influence the best troops to fight by our side with high morale and commitment. Troops that will execute such a strategy without hesitation and with great discretionary effort, all the while communicating frontline reality to leadership with the integrity required for leaders to make strategic decisions that actually change reality for the better.

Contrast Buford's decision and commitment with that of General Ewell of the Confederate army, who hesitated rather than fully commit to taking the high ground

A leader is never "practical" about taking and holding the high ground.

from the Union army when he had the opportunity in an early skirmish. Ewell was indecisive because General Robert E. Lee had ordered him to take the high ground "if practicable." In other words, a confounding leadership suggestion rather than a clear strategic imperative.

When leaders try to be practical, safe, or accommodating, rather than uncompromising in applying moral principles to their strategy, much energy, effort and expense is expended in battle, but with little impact, as evidenced by the thousands of dead and millions displaced in Ukraine. Many nations and organizations have lost their battles to survive, and countless numbers have died a slow death, the death of their souls, due to a lack of moral clarity, courage and decisiveness from their leaders in developing and articulating their strategy. Effective leaders never retreat from the high ground of moral clarity and uncompromising conviction in their strategy, decisions and communication, because they know the cost to those fighting alongside them. They understand that the lower moral ground produces low morale among the troops.

Famed nineteenth-century military strategist Carl von Clausewitz, a Prussian general who fought against Napoleon, wrote the book *On War*. It is regarded by military experts even today as a definitive study of warfare, and as you would expect contains many leadership lessons. In his chapter on "Moral Forces" Clausewitz wrote that "War is a trial of moral and physical forces by means of the latter. In the last analysis it is at moral, not physical strength, that all military action is directed ... *moral factors, then, are the ultimate determinants in war...* the effects of the physical forces and the moral are thus completely fused, and cannot be decomposed like a metal alloy by a chemical process."

His statements are validated by research cited earlier showing that the number one factor contributing to the loss of meaning and morale in organizations is when we are asked to do things that conflict with the higher universal moral values that influence us deeply. So when leaders ask soldiers or employees to act in conflict with these values, those who do so are effectively AWOL even if physically present due to the stress from their inner dis-ease and disintegration. This is reflected in the lack of morale and commitment in the young lads conscripted to serve in the Russian invasion of Ukraine, as well as in the low levels of commitment and engagement in many organizations.

Clausewitz also wrote that it is a "miserable philosophy made for fools" for a leader to ignore moral law and forces and then, "as soon as these forces make their appearance" (as they inevitably must), began to react as if they are a leader who is "a genius above all rules." A philosophy made for fools because moral and natural laws work 100% of the time, and natural law says that eventually we all will reap what we sow, no exceptions. Fortunately, we can put that law to work in our favor

Moral Law is Brutally Unforgiving...or Rewarding

and reap a bountiful harvest, rather than consider ourselves a genius above such rules and reap many painful lessons.

In *On War* Clausewitz also presents a thought-provoking description of the simplicity beyond complexity that characterizes effective strategy, but that proves elusive to most leaders for a variety of reasons that he elucidates. Among his thoughts are the following, which are worthy of serious reflection as they echo and reinforce many of the principles and subjects previously explored in this book:

> "It is still more ridiculous if, in addition to this, we reflect that the same critic, in accordance with prevalent opinion, excludes all moral forces from theory, and will not allow it to be concerned with anything but the material forces, so that all must be confined to a few mathematical relations of equilibrium and preponderance, of time and space, and a few lines and angles. If it were nothing more than this, then out of such a miserable business there would not be a scientific problem for even a schoolboy.

> Thus, then, in strategy everything is very simple, but not on that account very easy. Once it is determined from the relations of the state what should and may be done by war, then the way to it is easy to find; but to follow that way straightforward, to carry out the plan without being obliged to deviate from it a thousand times by a thousand varying influences, that requires, besides great strength of character, great clearness and steadiness of mind, and out of a thousand men who are remarkable, some for mind, others for penetration, others again for boldness or strength of will, perhaps

not one will combine in himself all those qualities which are required to raise a man above mediocrity in the career of a general.

It may sound strange, but for all who know war in this respect it is a fact beyond doubt, that much more strength of will is required to make an important decision in strategy than in tactics. In the latter we are hurried on with the moment; a commander feels himself borne along in a strong current, against which he durst not contend without the most destructive consequences, he suppresses the rising fears, and boldly ventures further. In strategy, where all goes on at a slower rate, there is more room allowed for our own apprehensions and those of others, for objections and remonstrances, consequently also for unseasonable regrets; and as we do not see things in strategy as we do at least half of them in tactics, with the living eye, but everything must be conjectured and assumed, therefore the convictions produced are less powerful. The consequence is, that most generals when they should act, remain stuck fast in bewildering doubts."

— **Carl Von Clausewitz**, *On War*, Book 3, Of Strategy in General, Chapter 1, Strategy

He goes on to say that "*The talent of the strategist is to identify the decisive point and to concentrate everything on it, removing forces from secondary fronts and ignoring lesser objectives.*" This is because no army or organization has unlimited resources, so for victory it is imperative to focus resources where there is the greatest potential for strategic advantage. Applying this definition to moral leadership is useful to help us understand how important the higher moral ground is to effective strategy, with the key lesson from Clausewitz being to identify and concentrate on the decisive point.

The Decisive Point of Concentration for Moral Leaders: People

"What a depth of devotion, sympathy and reassurance were conveyed through his smile."

These words were penned by a soldier from Wisconsin after meeting Lincoln in person. Lincoln met with about 2,000 soldiers individually during the Civil War after inviting any soldier with concerns or questions to meet with him. After one such meeting a soldier who had previously written that he had "never been in favor of the abolition of slavery" wrote that he was now "ready and willing" to fight for Lincoln's values and vision. "If he says that all slaves are forever free, Amen," wrote another. Many such sentiments were also expressed by the long lines of ordinary citizens lining the halls of the White House each day, most of whom Lincoln somehow found time to speak with.

The impact of Lincoln's people focus was a primary contributor to the shift that led from a fight to preserve the Union to the Emancipation Proclamation and ultimately a fight for freedom. Only about one third of the Union soldiers expressed a willingness to fight to free the slaves in the first year of the war, but after Lincoln declared the slaves free the vast majority of soldiers were willing to fight and die for emancipation. This trail of Lincoln's expanding influence also led to the eventual enlistment of over 200,000 black soldiers in the Union Army, men who played no small role in turning the tide of early Union defeats into ultimate victory. Moral leaders like Lincoln understand the power of a small ray of human sunshine to eventually change the entire picture.

Most leaders with some grand delusion of changing the world would not think any mere individual foot soldier worth

Antietam, Md., President Lincoln with Gen. George B. McClellan and group of officers. Selected Civil War photographs, 1861-1865 (Library of Congress)

a moment of their time. And if by chance encountering them, impatience or indifference would likely be the main impression conveyed. Lincoln's people focus, in contrast, was compelled both by his character and by his pragmatic understanding of how influence is spread far beyond our line of sight. It is spread primarily through the depth and integrity of countless individual encounters that ripple far beyond our personal reach, yet encounters with those possessing Lincoln's depth of integrity and sincere concern remain as unique and exceptional today as ever.

Lincoln's distinctly different view of the importance and worth of every single human he encountered was at the heart of his ability to influence in communication, as captured in his remarks to the Springfield Washington Temperance Society in 1842.

> *"If you would win a man to your cause, first convince him that you are his sincere friend. Therein is a drop of honey that catches his heart, which, say what he will, is the great highroad to his reason, and which, when once gained, you will find but little trouble in convincing his judgment of the justice of your cause, if indeed that cause really be a just one. On the contrary, assume to dictate to his judgment, or to command his action, or to mark him as one to be shunned and despised, and he will retreat within himself, close all the avenues to his head and his heart; and though your cause be naked truth itself, transformed to the heaviest lance, harder than steel, and sharper than steel can be made, and though you throw it*

with more than Herculean force and precision, you shall be no more be able to pierce him, than to penetrate the hard shell of a tortoise with a rye straw."[62]

Many of you, I suspect, would agree with me that many leaders upon reading these remarks would concentrate on how they might "convince" someone that they were indeed their sincere friend. It is clear from Lincoln's character, however, as well as a reading of the complete speech that his emphasis is upon "sincere." He is speaking of the importance of conveying what he assumes to be true, that is a sincere concern, rather than the leadership duplicity which convincingly feigns sincerity and empathy. Only true sincerity produces the "almost omnipotent" influence Lincoln possessed, as anything less is soon apparent. Lincoln, in ways I never could, describes well the defensive reactions of humans when we approach them rationally or emotionally, absent the leadership of our higher moral voice.

I heard the echoes of Lincoln when Fred Smith came to speak to a class of new frontline managers at the FedEx Leadership Institute. I was fortunate to be one of those new managers. "Why am I here today?" was his first question. With international expansion and rapid growth creating more strategic challenges than any CEO could deal with daily, he wanted us to know why he would spend an hour with a new class of young managers responsible for fifteen to twenty frontline employees when he could be meeting with senior leaders on multi-million-dollar issues.

There were two compelling reasons why he was there. First, he recognized the immense importance of frontline management, so he wanted to meet us in person to let us know how much he valued our roles. Second, he wanted us to understand the importance of keeping people as our decisive point of concentration, and he wanted to reinforce the importance of that strategic focus by showing up in person. It would be hard to overstate the enduring impact of his example on that one day throughout my career.

I also clearly recall him saying that by speaking to us in person he was potentially speaking to the thousands of employees we would be likely to encounter over our careers at FedEx. He understood the enormous leadership leverage that a decisive concentration on people, even with a small class of new frontline managers, would produce over the years to follow. Like the soldier from Wisconsin did for Lincoln, we spread the word far and wide about the integrity and power of Smith's example and sincere interest in us. And as with that soldier and Lincoln, it would be impossible to calculate the number of people whose values and priorities changed for the better, and whose loyalty and devotion deepened, as a result of one moment in time with such a leader.

Smith's strategic priorities at FedEx were always aligned with his vision of improving the lives of people, so it was natural that the decisive point upon which the company's strategy was focused was on its employees. More specifically toward applying the Golden Rule to everyone employed at FedEx by first prioritizing their job security, and then by investing in their continued job satisfaction and future growth and development. Our strategic priorities each year began with People, followed by Service and finally Profit related strategies.

Smith deeply believed that this prioritization was not only a moral imperative, but that people so treated would deliver the exceptional service required for sustained financial health. Over his fifty years as founder and CEO his track record speaks for itself. He never deviated nor was distracted by a thousand influences, as Clausewitz describes of most leaders, despite numerous economic downturns and other significant international market challenges. Training and development was sacred, rather than the first line item cut in a downturn.

This Golden Rule and people-first focus was not only a theme for the strategic prioritization of employees at FedEx, but then followed by its application to customers. I recall many a capital investment designed to make business easier, and service more reliable for customers, but which required years, and thus great faith in this moral principle to produce a return on investment. In the capital-intensive aviation and logistics business you do not make such investments without exceptional moral clarity and courage informing your strategy, nor without unwavering commitment to those golden principles no matter what winds of change or challenge may blow.

The key questions, then, are:

1. To what degree are people and the Golden Rule priori-
    tized and clearly reflected in your strategic planning
    and priorities?
2. How credible and durable is this golden thread as
    reflected in your daily investments and decisions?
3. And how easily are you distracted by lesser fronts and
    objectives?

I dare say there are more than a few leaders who have never
asked such questions, and whose internal challenges and market
results likely reflect this moral gap. Smith, like Clausewitz,
learned his lessons in leadership leading soldiers into battle,
and has carefully studied the art and nature of war, for within
it is distilled much timeless wisdom on strategy and human
nature. That is how he built a global leader and one of the
perennial top 10 most admired companies in the world with
a culture so loyal that employees talk about bleeding purple.

The pandemic has, of course, provided numerous examples
where any decisive focus on people and the Golden Rule was
missing in action from strategic priorities developed in the
executive suite,[63] and employees are responding precisely as
you would expect. There are thankfully some notable exceptions that have demonstrated the significant gap in employee
loyalty between companies whose leaders take the moral high
ground and those that do not.[64] It is remarkable to consider
the number of leaders whose strategy and related priorities
do not reflect the Golden Rule, yet who appear shocked and
dismayed at the rate at which they are losing critical talent.

As mentioned earlier in the book, the natural law of stimulus and response cannot be circumvented with lofty rhetoric about how much empathy a leader feels for those they had "no choice" but to let go, or how they were "forced to" reduce the training budget as their first option. There is an abundance of research demonstrating that this law works with the absolute reliability of gravity,[65] so why not chose the higher strategic path that puts this natural law to work in the best interest of everyone, including ourselves?

In *The Art of War* Sun Tzu wrote that war was a matter of life or death, a road either to safety or ruin. So is organizational leadership such a road, the resulting life and death that of human spirit and potential, and ultimately that of the enterprise. He attributed success or failure in war to five factors, the first of which he called The Moral Law. He defined it as the law that "causes the people to be in complete accord with their ruler, so that they will follow him regardless of their lives, undismayed by any danger."

The Moral Law causes people to be one with their leader, because Moral Law has been found to be universally present in the depths of the human heart, irrespective of any superficial differences. It is the deep well of our spirit where commitment, loyalty and discretionary effort reside, and can only be reached by a leader with moral clarity and courage. Leaders who operate by The Rational Law (basing decisions on futile attempts to calculate the odds or predict reactions), or The Emotional Law (feel-good strategies and rhetoric lacking any impact on reality), inevitably lead us down the road to ruin. But they often do so with furrowed brows and silver tongues for those that refuse to see any deeper. It may be a good time to start ruthlessly evaluating our leaders by The Moral Law, before we get to the end of a long and winding road and find ourselves at a dead end. Because moral factors are not only the ultimate determinants of victory or defeat in war as Clausewitz wrote, but also in business or any human endeavor.

Finally, Dr. King also provides a compelling example of how a leader living with moral integrity has the intellectual "free space" to create a unique and aligned people strategy that brings their vision to life. King's strategy, based on the higher principles of love and non-violence, was so unique that he once said, "…we shall have to create leaders who embody virtues we can respect, who have moral and ethical principles we can applaud with enthusiasm." This strategy was so integrated and aligned with his vision, due to his intellectual clarity born of leading from the moral high ground, that every march or activity leader had very clear guidelines on precisely how to execute his strategy in any scenario, no matter how challenging.

Despite enormous resistance and violence, Dr. King's army followed his non-violent guidelines with amazing consistency, even when resorting to more rationally or emotionally driven responses would have been understandable and even applauded by some. But his followers executed these guidelines under duress with incredible diligence and consistency due to the golden thread that ran from his vision through his strategy. In other words, the integrity of that thread was unquestionable, and the reason why Dr. King's leadership changed a nation. Anyone who aspires to have his leadership ability to see farther and higher enough to shape consensus, rather than search for it, can learn much from his example.

CHAPTER 9

Culture: Moral Leaders Take and Hold the High Ground

"I came to see, in my time at IBM, that culture isn't just one aspect of the game—it is the game."
— **Lou Gerstner**

"Society mandates compliance in business, but a business that raises the ethical bar beyond compliance elevates the standard for the entire industry."
— **Jamilia Grier, CEO at ByteBao**

"Culture eats strategy for breakfast" is often attributed to Peter Drucker, falsely so, as anyone who has read Drucker would know. Like emotional intelligence, culture has long been the focus of an extraordinary amount of thought and writing. Both have also been characterized as enormously challenging and difficult areas to master. Is it possible that much of the challenge is because both emotions and culture are end-of-process outcomes, and thus a myopic focus on them, rather than the process that produces them, leads to a reactive and never-ending struggle?

That process is defined by whether a leader has the moral clarity and courage to see a vision of the high ground in human endeavors, and then has the capability to develop a clear and compelling strategy to take and hold it. Culture, the beliefs, values and priorities that drive human behavior,[66] reflects how well a higher vision and strategy is preserved through the twists and turns of organizational relationships, functions, policy, structure, processes and performance management. Our leadership example, along with the strength and clarity of a higher vision and focused strategy, are the proactive and foundational components that make culture a far easier challenge to navigate.

To keep a golden thread intact through all the organizational twists and turns it is critical for leaders to have a "cultural ear." Just as a talented orchestra conductor has an exceptional musical ear that can detect a single note slightly off key, a single instrument a bit too loud, or a lack of perfect harmony and timing among musicians, effective leaders can quickly detect and proactively resolve the slightest deviations from a healthy and harmonious culture. Absent such leadership ability, employees inevitably create unwritten rules to compensate for any moral gaps in leadership, and to protect themselves as much as possible from the consequences of those gaps. Once these unwritten rules reach critical mass and become embedded in the culture, they not only significantly affect performance, but become increasingly costly and challenging to understand and address. Unwritten rules that initially produce hesitation, delay, internal battles, CYA behavior and duplicity in information sharing (as if that isn't enough), can quickly advance to include the sabotage of leadership efforts, whether intended or not.

Over my career I've encountered more than a few of these unwritten rules in businesses as diverse as logistics and healthcare. In one case packages with a 1 or 2-day delivery commitment were routinely delivered several days late to customers. Each of these packages showed up in online tracking information as attempted, but failed deliveries, due to the recipient not being at home. In reality the recipients had been at home, but some delivery drivers had been given such onerous workloads by management, and were working such long hours, that they had resorted to falsifying online information in an attempt to finish their shift with enough time remaining for a few hours of sleep. Repeated attempts to express their concerns to management had fallen on deaf ears, so this practice had spread among the workforce as a means to cope with excessive workloads, while also aimed at avoiding punitive management action for service failures.

These were not employees typically disposed to providing poor service, or to lying, which is what in essence they were doing. But while other options should have been used to elevate their concerns, their behavior is perfectly understandable. It is simply the law of stimulus and response at work once again. Why would they think that elevating their concerns would bring any resolution when local management was so lacking in integrity as to claim that people were their top priority, but then in their behavior and decisions clearly send the very opposite message?

"Don't say things. What you are stands over you the while, and thunders so that I cannot hear what you say to the contrary."
— In "Social Aims" by Ralph Waldo Emerson, 1875

I've found it typical of leaders in such toxic cultures that they do much more talking than leaders in healthy cultures, perhaps in the futile attempt to compensate for their hypocritical actions. Or perhaps they are delusional enough to believe they can fool people with their words. But contrast all their verbiage with a leader like Lincoln, whose most famous speech at a key moment in U.S. history, the Gettysburg Address, took less than two minutes and had only 272 words. He needed to say very little because of the moral clarity evident in his decisions and actions that preceded his words. Were it not for his prior leadership and decisive actions from the highest moral ground, his words would have had no credibility or influence at the time and would now be long forgotten. But because of the power of his example his words ring with sincerity and integrity, and the profound influence of those mere 272 words continues till this day.

Example

> *"Lead by example, not by talk. That's*
> *the mark of a great leader."*
> — Marshall Goldsmith, author of *The Earned Life*

Thus it is that a leader's example is not only the foundational requirement for a healthy and ethical culture, but also the most powerful component. Any words or directives that follow are no more, and thankfully no less, compelling than a leader's example. That, as I trust you have noted by now, is the focus of this book, and hopefully you are gaining some insight and inspiration to help you became a more compelling example of moral leadership. I have tried over the years to become more understated in my verbiage and to exceed expectations in my example, though to what degree I have achieved that others would be required to testify. I do think it a wise practice, as some leaders who promoted and lauded their so-called family cultures suddenly found their actions in conflict with any concept of family, and as a result were featured in the New York Times.[67] Far more challenging than such public exposure, however, is the mountain one needs to climb in order to restore any semblance of trustworthiness and credibility.

This book is designed to help you achieve this foundational trust and respect that others grant only to moral leaders. There are, of course, other areas important to building trust once this foundation is in place, and I recommend Joel Peterson's excellent book, *The 10 Laws of Trust: Building the Bonds That*

Make a Business Great, for an effective treatment of those areas. Trust is far more important than the shiny new objects many leaders become enamored with, as employees in high-trust organizations report 74% less stress, 50% higher productivity, 40% less burnout and 76% higher engagement than those in low-trust companies.[68]

To be a compelling example of moral leadership not only elicits trust, but such an example requires that we as leaders trust others as our default position, absent a compelling reason not to do so. That would seem to be a clear application of the Golden Rule. In our formative years, when our rational and moral capabilities were not fully developed, some of us learned to mistrust others (with good reason). If those people were key members of our family or social structure, it's likely that this mistrust was subconsciously hardwired into our synaptic patterns, and if we have not brought that reaction from an unconscious to conscious state, and modified it, it likely remains our initial protective response to others.

To mistrust by default was not as costly when things moved more slowly. Now it can be deadly since a lack of trust introduces skepticism, hesitation and delay into the execution of strategy. It also means we communicate with less candor and transparency, so we place others in positions where they cannot make effective decisions. These dynamics obviously breed a mutual mistrust that can quickly spiral into a self-perpetuating and crippling cycle in human relationships and organizational effectiveness, as is poignantly illustrated in the very different leadership approaches and results in the Russian and Ukraine militaries.[69] To initially trust by default not only accelerates execution and improves decision-making, one also learns much faster when there is a legitimate reason for distrust. And of course a wise leader knows how to set the proper boundaries that allow for initial trust, while avoiding the potential for irreparable damage with unknown people or scenarios. We are all good at expecting trust from others; it may be worth reflecting upon our example relative to extending trust and the kind of response that produces in others.

Alignment

It is imperative that leaders have their cultural ears attuned to the slightest discrepancy in organizational alignment that could signal a breach of integrity to employees. So attuned that hopefully any misalignment is identified and eliminated in the discussion phase and thus never implemented. Since you can develop a cultural EAR (my acronym using Example, Alignment, Review) through practice, here are three key areas of alignment focus that have a major impact on the moral nature and health of any culture.

Culture Fit, Add or Subtract?

A primary example of where severe and costly breeches of alignment occur between articulated values (whether written or spoken), and actual behavior, is in hiring and promotion decisions for employees and leaders. Especially when a leader's

157

short-term performance is given more weight in a promotion decision than their integrity and behavioral alignment with an organization's articulated values, a strong signal is sent to all employees, including other leaders, that those values are worth no more than the paper they are written on.

It is not hard to make this mistake given that performance is more easily quantifiable, and that the qualitative nature of values congruence is not only more challenging to evaluate, but takes more time to make its impact evident. It is that very nature, however, that makes it more insidious and corrupting to a culture over time. Performance deficiencies can be corrected far more easily and quickly than the toxic erosion of cultural values, an erosion that can easily reach an irreparable stage before its implications are recognized by senior leadership. Thus, the due diligence required to establish integrity and values congruence as the primary consideration in hiring and promotions is not optional to moral leadership, nor to ethical, healthy and resilient cultures. Many of you are likely familiar with the values-performance matrix, popularized by Jack Welch at GE, that addresses the critical importance of values alignment in hiring and promoting leadership talent. I recommend *The Culture Engine* by S. Chris Edmonds, and *Execution: The Discipline of Getting Things Done* by Larry Bossidy and Ram Charan, as guides for using this tool and excellent resources on building healthy cultures in general.

Culture fit, however, is increasingly under attack as outdated and a myth that undermines diversity, with cultural "add" being the new HR buzzword for more enlightened management.[70] This includes an HR Senior Vice President recently featured in a viral post on LinkedIn who said that to "disrupt the whole idea of culture fit, you should also acknowledge and recognize that all individuals are a culture add." Out of curiosity I looked at the Glassdoor reviews on this company, where it was immediately clear that what senior management added to their culture was primarily confusion, chaos and a lack of any coherent strategy or priorities. A sad but not at all shocking discovery.

When you compromise on a strong fit with your core values, you introduce beliefs and behaviors that are at odds with the value your customers pay for. These can "add" to your culture until it is so diluted and diverse that no one internally is able to clearly articulate anything unique or compelling about your organization. At which point your customers will have no idea what you stand for or why they should buy from you. The result is a self-perpetuating cycle of decline, the ultimate barrier to diversity since it eliminates all the new hiring and promotion opportunities that come only with strong performance and consistent growth.

I learned the value of culture fit at FedEx, for many years consistently ranked among the top 10 most admired companies in the world, just like Apple, where Steve Jobs was also adamant about culture fit. FedEx has also long been recognized, with numerous awards, as a leader in diversity in an industry where it has been notoriously difficult to achieve such leadership. I was fortunate to work for executives able to think critically enough about culture fit and diversity to see that placing them in opposition to one another is a false dichotomy. In reality, culture fit enhances diversity,[71] just as it does trust and a host of other positive cultural attributes required for organizational growth and success.[72] In fact, a review of the research just cited and working for a few years in any of the most admired companies in the world will clearly demonstrate how culture "add" (i.e. the ability to capitalize on each employee's ability to add new and innovative ideas that actually contribute to success) is only possible as a function of prior culture fit.

> *"These core values are the reason that Apple products have been so consistently excellent, and they are the reason that you can walk into any Apple store across the country and have essentially the same experience. From sales associates to top executives, Apple is united by a common culture. And it is that culture that ensures that Apple customers enjoy the experience that they have come to expect whenever they interact with Apple–whether that means using their iPhone, visiting an Apple store, or calling Apple's technical support line."*
> — **Fast Company**

Of course the concept of culture fit can be abused and applied inappropriately if you have immoral leaders perpetuating a toxic culture. But to cite exceptions, in the face of overwhelming examples and research showing the positive benefits, in order to posit a false dichotomy, is either naïve or disingenuous. I give the benefit of the doubt and assume the former, since those advocating these ideas tend to have no real world line management experience where they would have to face up close the execution chaos and confusion created by their new ideas. Every human is so unique and different that there is plenty of upside "add" left over after ensuring alignment with critical core values. To think that any human is a not only a good fit, but a positive add for a culture that has a Purple Promise[73] as a core value, or a "shared obsession with getting every last detail right"[74] is...well, I've already stated my perspective. But it is a way to get your senior leadership team mentioned often on Glassdoor.

A good way, in my experience, to assess for moral values and integrity fit in hiring and promotion is to inquire as to how people think generally, rather than to ask first for specific examples as the behavioral interview model indicates (leading questions tend to produce aligned answers). For example, two questions you may ask that will give you insight into a person's moral clarity and integrity would be:

1. How important is it to tell the truth in every situation? Is lying ever acceptable?
2. When should a leader practice the Golden Rule and why?

Asking these general questions gives a person wide latitude to show either their insight and wisdom relative to moral leadership, or their lack thereof. You may then inquire further along any lines of thought that would be helpful, as well as ask for examples that would show how closely their behavior aligns with their theory. Consider also these additional questions to ask that will help you evaluate moral values and integrity.[75] I dare say everyone has been in situations where withholding the full truth was the right application of the Golden Rule. But in such situations did they choose to lie, the emotionally easy option that further disintegrates our soular system, or simply choose to limit what they disclosed based on what was in the higher long-term interest of those affected? It does not take much time when you give people a broad playing field for them to demonstrate how they think relative to moral leadership, along with how well their thoughts and beliefs align with their actions.

> *"Every block of stone has a statue inside it; it's the task of the sculptor to discover it."*
> **– Michelangelo**

Finally, please allow me a brief word in favor of culture "subtract." When I began work at FedEx in my mid-twenties, and shortly afterward became interested in management, I quickly learned firsthand the value of cultural subtraction. By that I mean that FedEx had a process (LEAP: Leadership Evaluation and Assessment Process) and a class (Is Management for Me?) that identified beliefs, values and behaviors that I would have to subtract from my current notions about people and leadership before having any chance of being promoted into management at FedEx and aligning with Fred Smith's leadership philosophy and priorities. Giving up and leaving behind unproductive and less-than-moral values and priorities is an absolute prerequisite to adopting and executing higher and better values and behaviors. And I am forever grateful for the decade I spent in a culture that continually chipped away at the block of stone and challenged me to grow as a person and a leader.

Those with the bias and myopic vision required to advocate that culture "add" replace "fit" reflect a macro cultural shift that elevates individual self-expression as the ultimate source of meaning in life, rather than finding deeper meaning in conforming to higher moral values that advance the whole organization or society. But when individual expression is valued and rewarded as an "add," more so than the commensurate individual constraint (fit & subtract) required to enhance the whole, we should not be surprised to see the unraveling of a culture, organization or society into increasingly fragmented identities and groups until the whole loses any meaning and power of cohesion. Nor surprised to see the confusion, chaos and lack of strategic focus that precludes an organization from ever coming anywhere close to being one of the most admired companies in the world.

Effective leaders build a strong culture foundation on what can bind us together (universal moral values), rather than fracture us based on individual self-expression and superficial characteristics. What a wonderful opportunity leaders have to appreciate and capture the power of integrating culture fit, add and subtract to help employees become better people and leaders.

Onboarding

Onboarding is another example of a practice where values alignment is critical because this first impression of employees (to include the hiring experience) is a lasting and formative one. In my experience onboarding tends to primarily emphasize one of two important messages about the values and expectations of leadership. The first message is never explicitly stated of course, however, it is not hard to detect for a new employee.

1. You will be treated here as a disposable capital asset, expected to meet minimum standards, but we will not be surprised if you struggle and perhaps even fail. Thus you need to be aware of all the ways we will monitor you, of all the policies and procedures you need to comply with, and should we need to terminate you, how that will be done progressively and legally to ensure that we are not held liable, even though we may well have been complicit.

2. We recognize your unique and unlimited potential as a precious human soul. To help you reach your full potential, either here or elsewhere, we want you to know all the ways we will invest in you, and support you, to help your time with us be a richly rewarding learning and growth experience. And to prove that our behavior aligns with our values, we are going to begin that process now. In other words, we practice the Golden Rule beginning on day one.

Is it any wonder that the very same person, beginning with these two very different experiences, is almost guaranteed to behave and perform as two very different people, but in both cases, just as expected? Again, the immutable law of stimulus and response is at work, which in human relationships tends to produce self-fulfilling prophecies. Ritz-Carlton leadership understands the power of first and last impressions on both guests and employees, and provides a compelling and instructive example of the value and ROI of values alignment in onboarding, as well as learning and development in general.[76]

Performance Management

Since people tend to do what they are rewarded for, performance management and incentives are also key areas to watch for a lack of values alignment. In more than one instance I've heard senior leaders talk about how they prioritize high quality service and customer satisfaction in their culture. Yet, when talking, for example, to customer service agents in a call center, you find their compensation is tied primarily to their productivity. One does not need to ask whether their behavior reflects the priorities spoken by leadership or the realities of what they are rewarded for. This same dynamic would be expected in a culture where efficiency was valued over exceptional service, but employees were compensated based on customer satisfaction.

These seem such obvious examples that they are not worth citing, and yet such simple but egregious gaps in alignment between articulated values and actual organizational practice have appeared too many times to dismiss. More than once I've found management evaluations, incentives and metrics that rewarded leadership competition in areas where collaboration was both the stated and needed value. In one case our client, a major airline, had incentives for local hub on-time performance that produced system-wide lost luggage, stranded passengers and many customer complaints. The simple realignment of incentives with stated values played a major role in that airline quickly moving from last to second in FAA on-time performance rankings.

It takes only one such gap for the integrity and credibility of leadership to be questioned, and ultimately dismissed, if the lack of alignment is not quickly repaired. And talented people who recognize these gaps are likely to still act in ways that diminish the health and performance of the whole system if they are otherwise incentivized and rewarded. Sometimes the easiest and most obvious areas where lack of alignment and integrity exist have the greatest ROI.

Review

Given human imperfections and organizational complexities, leaders must have a mechanism to help them consistently review a culture. A culture constitution, along with regular reviews of compliance and gaps relative to that constitution, can be invaluable as a tool to help leaders identify both cultural strengths and gaps that need to be addressed. Once again, I recommend *The Culture Engine* by S. Chris Edmonds as a guide for developing and implementing an effective constitution for your organization. My only counsel would be to use verbs as much as possible to describe values (e.g. "always tell the truth" vs. "honesty"),[77] as this greatly increases both clarity and impact for people.

The predominant beliefs, values and behaviors within a culture are simply aggregated from a group of humans, so the fact that our individual brain adapts to each act of dishonesty by reducing our emotional signals of guilt, as previously cited, means that any culture is also subject to this same slippery slope of moral deterioration. In fact, a culture can slide into lower moral territory more quickly due to the collective reinforcement that occurs in reaction to either lower leadership behavior or influence among employees. Thus, the need for a finely tuned cultural ear and proactive corrective actions by senior leadership. Otherwise, even the most positive and noble cultural values can produce shadow behaviors when leaders fail to recognize the full implications of their actions and decisions.[78]

There are now over two decades of research[79] informing us how ethical cultural deterioration occurs. It begins with moral disengagement,[80] which is the process of suppressing our moral voice and engaging in lower moral behavior to the degree that we start the cycle of rationalization, outsourcing of blame and victimization described earlier in this book. Once there are enough employees on this path to produce a critical mass of influence within the culture, you can be sure enough damage has been done to require a major investment of time and leadership effort in order to restore an ethical culture. So it is critical to have a cultural ear that picks up the signs of this ethical deterioration in any review process. Those signs include:

1. *Reduced moral self-awareness*: This is to be expected when leadership prioritizes short-term profit or other operational goals to the extent that employees feel pressured or incentivized to take moral shortcuts to appease management, and begin to ignore their higher moral voice and values. Thus a moral leader needs to heighten the sensitivity of their cultural ear when change or performance pressures are increased within their team or organization.

2. *Reduced alignment of one's soular system*: If employees do not respond to guilt and correct their behavior, they inflict permanent damage on their soular system and accelerate its dis-integration. They no longer reflect deeply upon or discuss the moral implications of decisions or actions with other members of the culture, thereby mitigating any healthy cultural norms that previously prevented such action through collective influence. When such conversations do not regularly and informally occur, a moral leader recognizes that this may signal further moral deterioration of the culture.

3. *New cultural narratives*: New stories reach a critical mass of influence within a culture, replacing healthy stories and

norms. These stories ignore long-term moral implications to focus instead on rational or emotional justifications for unethical behavior (required to keep my job, we are all in this together, not illegal, etc.), and include victim narratives that exonerate any employees involved, while laying full responsibility on leadership as the sole perpetrators and participants in unethical behavior.

The best way to be attuned to these signals is to rely on informal ethical leaders that have their ear to the ground and pick up on these signals before management becomes aware of them. To do that these informal leaders need to be involved in ethically focused conversations with management on a regular basis as part of any review process. My reliance on these informal leaders was a key to my success in two major operational turnarounds that led to my nomination to the FedEx Leadership Institute, and has been highlighted by CEO's who led major change efforts as a key to their success.[81]

In every case of moral cultural decay there have been clear signs in management communication that the organization was ethically deteriorating, on average more than six years before any scandals made news headlines.[82] Extensive MIT research into what produces toxic cultures found that the two top contributors were a lack of leaders practicing the Golden Rule in their treatment of others and unethical management behavior.[83] Thus, there is no shortage of early warning signals to moral leaders who wish to build and sustain ethical cultures, nor is there a shortage of evidence (already cited in Part 1) that such cultures greatly outperform those where leaders are otherwise focused.

But the early signs of ethical decay are viewed as insignificant and justifiable by too many leaders, as in the case of a company whose sales leadership began to count sales that had closed, but not yet been paid, as revenue. Only a couple of years later, after several other "insignificant" decisions designed to inflate public perception of their performance, they were placing bricks into boxes, hoping that they would be counted as hard drives by government inspectors of inventory.[84] Any leader seeing the future moral implications of every decision, as did Lincoln, could have easily predicted and avoided this outcome from that first decision.

You will find at the other end of the ethical leadership spectrum, including cases where major culture change was the goal, that the most successful leaders focused on leadership examples and accountability, aligning policies and processes with articulated values, and on building relationships with informal leaders who had strong influence and leverage within the culture.[85] They focused first on small changes to build critical mass and support for a compelling vision and strategy: compelling because a golden thread, woven on higher moral ground, was clearly evident. Resistance quickly fades and positive energy builds naturally for such leaders, because they are tapping into the deepest universal well of self-transcendent values.

This well is so powerful that in each of the references cited above these successful leaders never announced a major "culture change" initiative (sure to be interpreted defensively by employees as "we" need to change). Instead, they understood the power of higher leadership examples, organizational alignment and sharply tuned cultural ears to naturally produce a highly supportive and engaged response. This is a much simplified approach compared to the onerous culture change initiatives you will find attempted in many organizations, with marginal to no performance impact evident even after years of costly effort. And a simplified approach that produces meaningful results in less time, as evidenced not only in the cases cited above, but in one of our leadership development clients who turned around a 50-million-dollar revenue shortfall to become the first division within the company to exceed 100 million dollars in EBITDA, all within 18 months.

FedEx Culture and Diversity as a Model

As mentioned previously, FedEx has been internationally recognized many times as a model company for its culture (as a best place to work, best employer, etc.) as well as for diversity and inclusion.[86] The diversity and inclusion achievements of the company, from its Board of Directors through all levels of management and beyond, are not only remarkable given its industry, but confounding to some given that the company's Chief Diversity Officer is also the Senior Vice President of the Eastern U.S. Operating Division of FedEx Express. Confounding due to the lack of a discreet office and functional bureaucracy devoted exclusively to diversity and inclusion. But those who understand the fundamental necessity and power of example, alignment and review, however, understand that often formal bureaucracies and programs are constructed in attempts to compensate for gaps in moral leadership, a futile and frustrating undertaking.[87] Compensating for skills deficiencies with functional experts is understandable, but deeper moral issues must be proactively and inextricably woven into an organization's hiring and development strategy at every level, with ownership for execution fully assumed by line management.

Thus, diversity at FedEx has always simply been a natural extension of the People First strategy, which calls for treating each human with the respect and dignity they deserve, and as part of that respect working to provide equal access and capability readiness for internal opportunities. If you read interviews with Shannon Brown, for many years now a key senior HR, diversity and line executive at FedEx, you will find his keys to leading the successful diversity efforts at FedEx are far more proactive and strategic than what you often hear from similar leaders.[88] From the earliest days of FedEx, Fred Smith ensured that the golden thread of his People First philosophy was integral to any FedEx strategic plans and priorities as previously outlined. The leadership examples of this philosophy in action, the alignment of policies and processes (for example, the employee development process and the promotion from within policy that Brown discusses in the cited interview), and the annual review of how well this People First approach is being executed have naturally embedded diversity and inclusion into the DNA of the FedEx culture.

In contrast to this proactive and strategic approach, many organizations and diversity leaders focus their efforts on the micro dissection of people into ever increasing numbers of identity groups, based on superficial characteristics, rather than on uniting people based on common universal values like the Golden Rule. Given the natural law of stimulus and response, it should come as no surprise that people react defensively and unproductively when so prejudicially judged,[89] no matter their race. And no surprise that as research grows on these typical approaches that their ineffectiveness and unintended consequences become more compelling.[90] Hopefully approaches like that of Chloe Valdary,[91] that begin and end with love and respect, will continue to gain attention and momentum based on their success (I recommend you listen to Simon Sinek's podcast with Chloe if you wish to ground diversity in moral principles with positive and sustainable impact).[92]

Culture, as a composite of individual uniqueness and relationships, has one chance to be a powerful and coherent force for human growth and business success. And that chance is to be grounded in what all unique humans have in common, the universal moral values strong enough to forge unbreakable bonds, focus us beyond our differences and enable us together to overcome any challenge.

CHAPTER 10

Intuition and Decision-Making

Intuition

"Intuition is a very powerful thing,
more powerful than intellect."
— Steve Jobs

There is now substantial research indicating the value and effectiveness of intuitive decision making. Intuition has long been generally regarded as an inferior approach to more structured critical thinking and analysis. Yet, as our world has become more volatile, uncertain and complex, the speed of decision making has risen in importance. Markets and operating environments now relentlessly punish those who may be right, but late, with strategic decisions. And by the time you develop all the environmental and market data required for a thorough critical analysis, that data may no longer be accurate or relevant enough to produce a decision that leads rather than lags the market.

But unfortunately, intuitive decision making has often been characterized as a function of the "gut," i.e. more emotional than rational or moral. Researchers at the Max Planck Institute for Human Development in Berlin, however, found that intuition is a vastly under-appreciated form of unconscious, but learned, intelligence.[93] It is thus neither irrational nor absent a grounding in knowledge in its effective form; it is simply the ability to access critical thinking and knowledge without the time or conscious process normally required.

It is therefore essential to understand how we can develop this unconscious, faster and effective form of decision making, and its relationship to our soular system and higher moral voice. There are two foundational requirements for us to develop this critical leadership advantage.

Become Insatiable Learners and Critical Thinkers

Sound intuitive ability is the product of prior rigorous learning and thinking that eventually enables us to become unconsciously competent at making good decisions. Thus, when time and the scenario allows, it is critical to practice, refine and continually improve our critical thinking and analysis skills, for these are the genesis of sound intuition. Jeff Bezos is an example of how practicing critical thinking creates sound intuition. He has stated that, *"All of my best decisions in busi-ness and in life have been made with heart, intuition, guts... not analysis."* Bezos is also, however, a rigorous critical thinker as can be seen from Amazon's 14 principles and the unique way he conducts meetings to ensure that there is critical thinking and analysis before input. His decision to buy the Washington Post is a good example of how critical thinking and intuition can work together effectively in leaders, but with intuition playing the key role.[94]

It would be an understatement to say that Einstein was a gifted mathematician and critical thinker, yet his greatest breakthroughs, including his special theory of relativity, came from his intuition and imagination. An intuition so powerful and effective because of his relentless passion for learning and critical thinking, a passion born of and sustained by his humility. Humility is at the heart of the constant quest to keep learning and to think more critically in leaders that enjoy strong and accurate intuition: humility from the recognition of how much they do not know, no matter how much they may have learned. Einstein's statement that "I have no special talents, I am only passionately curious," stands in stark contrast to so many today eager to label themselves as gurus, experts, thought leaders, or influencers.

Humility, in contrast, makes us eager to hear other ideas and perspectives, leads us to quickly admit mistakes, improve our thinking when wrong, and prevents us from becoming so enamored with the sound of our own voice that we begin to believe that we can actually learn something new by hearing ourselves talk. Even a cursory review of the life of Einstein will produce many surprising examples of humility, with an unmistakable correlation to his passion for constantly learning and for improving his thought processes, and thus his intuition.[95] These prerequisites to critical thinking,[96] constant learning and humility, produce cerebral agility so that our synaptic connections fire far more quickly, effectively and unconsciously than in others.

Create Cerebral Free Space

No matter how much we may have learned, if our unconscious operating system is polluted, contaminated and fragmented, we have no chance of being either fast or right with our intuition. And the primary way we pollute and fragment our cerebral free space is when we violate our moral compass, because then we are compelled to continually seek to justify our wrong behavior. Since our conscience will not allow that, we fill our cerebral free space with stress, guilt, toxic emotions and neural storms that cripple our creative, critical thinking and decision-making abilities. fMRI's literally show our brain closing synaptic pathways (e.g., between the prefrontal cortex and limbic systems) from this stress, just as we would close a door when noise from another room is interfering with our meeting. Not only are our unconscious intuitive abilities now crippled, even our conscious efforts at decision making have no chance to be either fast or effective. It's the equivalent of trying to think deeply in an over-crowded, over-heated, noisy and stressful office...only much worse because removing that toxicity from our brain is much harder than finding a new working space.

Martin Luther King Jr. provides a timeless example of how living by high moral values, and with a clear conscience, enables us to unconsciously, intuitively and quickly make decisions that align with our purpose and strategy, even in extremely volatile and challenging scenarios. MLK made a number of unconventional and surprising decisions (e.g. refusal to endorse a political party or candidates), driven by his intuition, that reflected an intellectual clarity and depth that only someone with a clear conscience can possess.[97] This is the same unique and powerful leadership ability that enabled Lincoln to intuitively request the Marine band to play Dixie when the crowd demanded that he make a speech on the eve of his Civil War triumph.

I love aviation, so Richard Branson also comes to mind as a good illustration of the link between moral integrity and intuitive decisions within a business context. He has often, even at the Vatican, shared his views on why he believes "leaders need morality, and humility, at heart." After spending a night in jail in his youth for a tax evasion scam at Virgin records, he vowed never again to do anything for which he would feel embarrassment or guilt (this after his mother bailed him out of jail). No embarrassment, no guilt, and no related stress, so plenty of cerebral free space to make effective intuitive decisions.

In fact, the decision to launch Virgin Atlantic in 1984, with the significant risks of selling Virgin Records, while also taking on the monopoly of British Airways was a decision made with Branson's intuition rather than through any structured analysis.[98] And it is hard to keep up with the number of successful businesses and ventures he has created in his career since then, all credited to his intuition. Both Branson and MLK validate this correlation between a clear conscience and intuitive decision making, as well as the importance of lifelong learning. No one who has read MLK doubts for a moment his knowledge and scholarship. And Branson has repeatedly said that one of his most important values is "to always be learning, no matter your age."

A strong body of research and compelling leadership examples now illustrate how we can make effective decisions driven primarily by our intuition, or unconscious intelligence. The foundational checklist to place us on this path is fairly simple and straightforward to understand, but much harder to do. My hope is that through moral clarity and courage you can create the cerebral free space and strong foundation to advance your intuitive capability and avoid the "junk in = junk out" trap that corrupts any intuitive advantages.

It should go without saying that there is certainly a time and place when structured decision making, based on rigorous critical analysis, should be the primary driver of decisions, and good leaders know that. However, as the world moves faster and we rely more on analytics and AI to make decisions, we risk losing the creativity, reasoning and imagination born only from human intuition. And as Branson reminds us, *"these will be the soft leadership skills in highest demand in the future."* No longer just a luxury, using intuition to make faster and better decisions is increasingly a requirement for business survival and success, and a healthy soular system is the essential foundation for that capability.

Decision-Making

On the morning of Jan. 28, 1986, I was standing just across the bay from the launch pad, my eyes fixed on the Challenger space shuttle rocketing into a deep blue sky when it exploded only 73 seconds into flight. That surreal experience led me to research how such a tragic decision could have been made.

To my shock I found that problems with the O-rings (gaskets) that failed were well known from prior shuttle flights and lab tests. In fact, the explosion and death of 6 astronauts and the first teacher in space was almost a certainty given the unusually cold temperature at launch, although the data was never organized or presented in a way to establish that until after the tragedy. However, five of the booster rocket engineers from Morton-Thiokol (MTI) were convinced of the extraordinary risk and presented their case with charts and arguments on the evening prior to and the morning of the launch.

Of course the NASA bias was strongly in favor of a launch, after all, that's their mission. The launch had been scheduled, then canceled, for several days so internal pressure was great to finally go. This bias resulted in hurried meetings the evening before the launch, inadequate time to present and review arguments, hasty preparation of charts, and offline conversations that should have involved all key players. It is a case study for what Peter Drucker called the most critical skill for executives, decision-making. Decisions produce shifts in organizational priorities and resource allocation, drive cultural norms and unwritten rules, and often have significant unintended consequences. In this case, as with the Edmund Fitzgerald and Boeing 737 MAX scenarios, deadly ones.

Here are some key leadership lessons from this tragic decision that relate directly to a healthy soular system and our higher moral voice:

Establish Clear Parameters and Value Priorities

In *The Effective Executive* Drucker wrote about the morning the New York Times printed only half the usual number of papers because an editor and staff had argued for nearly an hour over the correct way to hyphenate a single word. Since executives had made it clear that the paper set the standard for written English, printing the paper with a possible error was a sacred line never to be crossed. Thus, it was an easy decision to take a hit on circulation and revenue for that day, rather than risk making a single mistake.

Had NASA management had a Golden Rule launch decision parameter that adding any additional risk to the safety of the astronauts was unacceptable, those precious lives would have been saved. Priorities, investments and behaviors change when leaders make decisions. Thus, it is imperative that everyone in management be clear on the decision parameters and the relative prioritization between values like revenue, people, speed and quality. Because decisions send a powerful message, far more so than words, echoing through the halls of an organization about what is really important. Especially about whether lofty concepts like the Golden Rule and integrity are foundational principles that hold up under pressure, or only as fragile as the paper they are written on. Most of the stress, ineffectiveness and unintended consequences of decisions can be eliminated by proactively creating moral value parameters and priorities, and then evaluating your proposed decision by how well it aligns with and supports those.

Develop Mechanisms to Protect Against Your Bias

A mechanism is something simple to implement that happens automatically, with the commitment to never dismiss or circumvent it. NASA could have easily had a mechanism that canceled a launch and required an unhurried and orderly review process, led by a safety expert, anytime a credible party raised a serious safety concern. In the absence of such a mechanism, however, NASA's bias to launch led them to challenge the safety concerns of MTI management and ask them to reconsider. MTI management, given the importance of the NASA contract, caved to this pressure and withdrew their no launch recommendation. In other words, the process in this case was one that reinforced the inherent NASA bias, rather than one that checked it.

My decision bias under pressure is to make decisions that avoid any significant or immediate hurt to anyone, even if that may not be in the best long-term interest of the entire team or organization. My mechanism to protect against extending this bias beyond its useful and moral limits is to call a long-time colleague, who does not have this bias, to get a different perspective before I make any major people decisions. It is far more effective to have such a mechanism in place than it is to try and figure out by yourself whether your bias is working as a positive or negative factor in each scenario.

Lincoln seems also to have had a people bias that exceeded useful limits on a few occasions. The most notable example was his long tolerance of General McClellan (Army of the Potomac) despite his repeated failures to pursue Lee aggressively, his retreats even when he had superior numbers, his direct refusal to obey Lincoln's orders and his lack of support for the Emancipation Proclamation. It is noteworthy that Lincoln chose as his replacement Ambrose Burnside, a much more aggressive General, who shortly afterward cost the Union thirteen thousand dead and wounded soldiers in reckless attacks on Lee at the Battle of Fredericksburg.[99] To fail to understand our decision biases, and develop mechanisms to mitigate them, tends to cascade into multiple poor and costly decisions as we overreact in attempts to compensate for our prior mistakes.

Just be sure if your mechanism is another person, rather than a checklist or process, that they have their soular system and moral compass in good working order in the event your system gets unbalanced. That does not seem to be the case with the NASA leader responsible for the launch decision as during his limited discussion with MTI engineers he asked, "My God Thiokol, when do you want me to launch, next April?"[100] That seems to reflect a soular system being influenced by outside pressures, likely due to the multiple cancellations, rather than one where a clear rational mind and calm emotions are producing sound critical thinking under the leadership of a healthy moral voice.

Facilitate Dialogue, Not Just Debate

As Peter Senge pointed out in The Fifth Discipline, teams will often produce worse decisions than an individual due to the complexity of team dynamics. In the absence of effective leaders with a healthy soular system a bad decision is a very likely team outcome. From numerous first-hand accounts it is clear there was at best a discussion, and plenty of debate, but little if any leadership facilitation of a learning dialogue around the NASA launch decision. People moved in and out of the process, sidebars developed, the MTI engineers were at times excluded and even had to interrupt management to shove their charts back in front of them. This "process" had no chance of producing a dialogue, characterized by questions and inquiry more than advocacy, that would facilitate the learning required for a good decision.

The discussion of whether to launch or not quickly deteriorated and lost any chance of becoming a learning dialogue when, according to one of the Thiokol engineers later interviewed, NASA pressure resulted in Thiokol leadership "putting their management hats back on." Unfortunately, putting a management hat on seems too often to result in a cold rational approach to decision making that excludes the larger human picture, as well as anyone trying to bring that perspective to the debate. An effective leader welcomes dissent and contrarian points of view, ensures that they are fully considered, and is most concerned when everyone is in full agreement.

As Alfred Sloan, the executive who led the rise of GM from the 1920's to the 50's once famously said at the end of a meeting, "Gentlemen, I take it we are all in complete agreement on the decision here. Thus, I propose we postpone further discussion of this matter until the next meeting to give ourselves time to develop disagreement, and perhaps gain some understanding of what the decision is all about." In the NASA discussions these dissenting views were initially present, but they were quickly marginalized, then excluded from the process by those who were supposed to be leading an effective decision-making session. Certainly no one at NASA wanted to kill six of their own, along with the first teacher into space, on that cold January morning. Yet they ensured precisely that very outcome with their ineffective leadership by not welcoming, exploring, and even demanding dissenting viewpoints. The humility and big picture perspective produced by a healthy soular system enables a leader to not only welcome, but solicit dissent in the pursuit of learning, rather than seek the immediate emotional pleasure that comes with agreement and consensus.

Once again Lincoln provides a compelling example of the leadership wisdom that ensures disparate views are not only at the decision-making table, but effectively engaged and respected. After winning the 1860 presidential election Lincoln appointed his bitter political rivals, the three men who had challenged him for the presidential nomination (William Seward, Salmon Chase, and Edward Bates), to the top positions in his cabinet. These three had not only been vociferous and at times downright mean in their personal attacks on Lincoln, but were notorious for their acrimonious relationships among themselves, some of them even unwilling to enter a building if they knew one of the others was present.

Lincoln's rationale for this unconventional decision was that he had looked the party over and concluded that these were the strongest men for these critical roles, and that he had no right to deprive the country of their services. His wisdom in selecting this *Team of Rivals* (the title of Doris Kearns Goodwin's book that won the Lincoln Prize for its in-depth exploration of this subject) was validated many times over. Seward, for example, challenged Lincoln's planned timing of

Francis Carpenter's famous painting of Lincoln with his cabinet,
First Reading of the Emancipation Proclamation. *Carpenter studied
and sketched Lincoln for nearly seven months in 1864.*

the Emancipation Proclamation during a series of military
defeats, contending that the announcement would be far
better received by the public after a major victory. "It was an
aspect of the case that, in all my thought upon the subject, I
had entirely overlooked," Lincoln later stated.[101] Seward was
also instrumental in keeping the European nations, especially France, from recognizing the Confederacy and further
complicating the path to victory for the Union. Numerous
examples illustrating the value of Lincoln's wisdom in bringing
these disparate perspectives together to debate "first the one
side and then the other of every question arising"[102] abound
in Goodwin's book as well as in the other sources listed in the
Lincoln bibliography I provide.

Have the Courage to Make the Right Decision and Take Meaningful Action

"U.S. studies Ukraine war options" was a news headline I read a few days ago, nearly four months after the Russian invasion of Ukraine began. These four months later the Russian ruble is at a 7-year high against the U.S. dollar, smashing all previous records. China is buying twice as much oil from Russia as in previous years, adding billions to the Russian treasury. Meanwhile, a country has been flattened with over 10,000 civilian casualties (4,500 dead including over 300 children).

This is what happens when indecisive leaders, driven by their rational and emotional dimensions, keep delaying decisions while trying to calculate all possible stakeholder, friend and enemy reactions (a futile task), all the while basking in the immediate emotional comfort of doing enough to make them feel good, but not enough to alter reality in any meaningful way. Zelensky, in contrast, was immediately and convincingly decisive in his leadership, staking out the moral high ground and holding it. When offered evacuation by the U.S. to rush him away from Kyiv when the invasion started, Zelensky refused, saying, "The fight is here. I need ammunition, not a ride."

General Mark Milley, the U.S. Chairman of the Joint Chiefs of Staff, when giving the 2022 commencement address at West Point said, "Yet again in Ukraine we are learning a lesson that aggression left unanswered only emboldens the aggressor." Many of the most credible military experts, including General Jack Keane and Dan Rice,[103] President of

Thayer Leadership at West Point and Special Advisor to the Ukrainian Commander-in-Chief General Valeriy Zaluzhnny, have written extensively about early missed opportunities in the first few days of conflict when it quickly became evident how unreliable Russian equipment was, along with how low the morale of their troops. Sadly, indecisive leadership has not only led to much preventable death and destruction, but such leadership continues these many months later.[104]

I was privileged to work for a decisive leader, Frederick W. Smith, founder/CEO of FedEx, who said, "When people ask what principles have guided me since I started FedEx 35 years ago, my answer often startles them: It's the leadership tenets that I learned in the U.S. Marine Corps." Smith was a Platoon Leader, out in front risking his life in battle. In battle you either correctly assess reality, rather than suffer from delusions or paralysis by analysis, and then act decisively, or you die along with those you lead. I heard him say several times that no decision is a decision, and almost always the wrong decision. That is especially true when moral clarity and courage are required and much is at stake. It is precisely in such moments that we expect, and rightly so, for a leader to have a higher moral perspective than others and take decisive action.

Moral clarity, courage and decisiveness are the most compelling and influential attributes a leader can possess. This is evidenced by the thousands of Ukraine citizens that waited in line for weapons and a ride to the fighting lines. And by the many FedEx employees who talk about "bleeding purple." No surprise given Smith's decisive commitment to his People First philosophy when his ZapMail initiative was shut down, resulting in the immediate redundancy of 1,300 employees, all of whom were absorbed without a single furlough at a significant short-term cost to the company. While many leaders have been willing to sacrifice the jobs of those in their self-described "family" cultures to protect their short-term financial interests, leaders like Zelensky and Smith never need to do a cost/benefit analysis, take a poll or call a meeting to decide how to live their values.

Lincoln repeatedly demonstrated how decisive he could be, perhaps no more so than as the election for his second term was approaching in the summer of 1864. After the Union victory at Gettysburg Lee had regrouped and defeated Grant's army at Spotsylvania, Cold Harbor and Petersburg. As the number of Union casualties climbed to over 500,000 (with over 50,000 of those during the summer of 1864) the public sentiment for a peace deal with the Confederacy gained strong momentum. Republican National Committee chairman Henry Raymond advised Lincoln to set aside his commitment to emancipation and seek peace talks only around the issue of reunification, informing Lincoln that "the tide is setting strongly against us" and that a compromise was his only chance for reelection.[105]

To which sentiment Lincoln replied that he would rather face defeat than fail to keep his promise regarding emancipation, believing that he "should be damned in time and in eternity" should he compromise his integrity.[106] Note that he did not say that he would be, but that he "*should be...*" How many leaders today have that depth of moral clarity and conviction? These are the fine distinctions in leadership perspective that most pass over without notice, but as with Lincoln's equating the accidental telling of the truth with a lie, this depth of moral awareness separates those leaders who achieve almost omnipotent influence from those who will never approach it.

As adamant as Lincoln was to hear disparate viewpoints on many issues, when integrity and fixed moral principles were at stake he was absolutely uncompromising in his moral clarity and courage. As a result, the President swept the Electoral College in the subsequent election by a tally of 212 to 21 votes. Those who voted for him, especially the soldiers, transcended their self-interest by voting for principles that would extend the war rather than for a compromise that could bring peace.

Every leader will many times make the choice between "expert" or conventional wisdom and the moral high ground. The experts who try to gauge the winds and then adjust their moral sails are always astounded when the rare leader like Lincoln comes along and defies all expectations and predictions. But when a leader has the moral clarity and courage to touch and awaken the self-transcendent values divinely embedded in every human heart, why would anyone expect otherwise?

The Decisive Cost of "Too Much" Empathy and Emotional Intelligence.

How did we arrive at a point where there are a dearth of leaders with moral decision-making clarity and courage? In part by creating cultures at many levels that value soothing words and emotions above confronting harsh realities with morally courageous decisions and actions. These cultures are the inevitable outcomes of elevating "self" and feelings as the ultimate forms of self-expression and meaning, while diminishing the value of any decisive action in the service of universal values that some dare to presume higher and fixed.

I've seen many articles and comments applauding leaders for their emotional intelligence because they so eloquently expressed empathy for the workers they were laying off. This applause for the verbal expression of their feelings in spite of the huge integrity gap between their decisions and their prior words of loyalty and commitment to those they often referred to as "family." Just google "CEO empathy layoffs" to see how much our culture applauds so-called empathy and emotion laden rhetoric, instead of questioning the hypocrisy of leadership decisions in self-proclaimed family cultures. Or review all the empathy rhetoric from world leaders for Ukraine, absent the decisive action and support required to make a real difference in the outcome. Or ask people posting or demonstrating for peace, or displaying a Ukraine flag, what charity they donated to given their deep empathy for the cause.

This leadership phenomenon is not surprising given the elevation of emotions we discussed earlier and the related cultural shift that underlies it. This primary and narrow focus on emotions fails to account for the fact that any emotion has useful limits beyond which unintended and unproductive consequences begin to occur. Empathy is a compelling example of this given its popular connotations, typically including the ability to feel and mirror the emotions of others, in reaction to which I offer for your consideration the following observations:

1. I don't want someone to imagine how I am feeling or what I am thinking, although it may be helpful to inquire about my scenario so they can offer or refer me to help. Unless they have the same life history and have been in precisely the same scenario, with the same personality, beliefs and values as me, what chance do they have to think or feel as I do?

2. I don't want someone to mirror my feelings, because to do that they would first need to fully understand them (see #1). I would appreciate them helping me to better understand the root causes of my feelings so I can channel them into productive action, or change them when they are counterproductive.

Who wouldn't be overwhelmed by the futility and effort required to try and achieve everything included in these popular concepts of empathy? In fact in a graphic gone viral multiple times "feeling overwhelmed" is included as part of the definition of empathy. It is no wonder that the word has such nebulous meaning and boundaries, as it has only been in use in the English language since the early 20th century. But as so defined empathy becomes a black hole drawing us inward until we are unable to escape our own feelings, in the process draining our energy and weighing us down until we are paralyzed.

What is not nebulous, from my humble perspective, is that relative to moral leadership decisiveness, empathy as popularly defined can:

1. Easily become virtue signaling that turns into virtue substitution, i.e., the tendency to feel moral and good about ourselves because we feel (and talk) so much "empathy." Have you considered that the weight of all that empathy we feel may in fact be the unconscious guilt we accrue when we substitute emotions for meaningful leadership decisions and action?

2. Lead to poor decisions when we identify too much with others. When people were asked to evaluate the capabilities of a blind person by simulating their condition, they vastly underestimated their capabilities and potential. In a time of acute stress, like many have recently experienced, those in anxious and stressed states of mind will typically underestimate their capabilities and potential. I ask the rhetorical question, what is the moral leader's responsibility in such a scenario if they are practicing the Golden Rule?

3. Erode moral clarity and courage in decisions while also eroding the ethical fabric of a culture, as multiple studies in decision-making and behavioral science have demonstrated.[107] Many of us have firsthand knowledge of family cultures where integrity unraveled, enabling decisions were made, and destructive emotional triangles were formed due to empathy as often defined and

practiced. The same dynamics work in any culture, the impact simply appears more gradually at scale.

4. Cause leaders to make decisions that adapt themselves and their organizations to their most immature, recalcitrant, and anxious members, rather than to "the energetic, the visionary, the imaginative, and the motivated."[108] It is hard to imagine a more egregious leadership violation of the Golden Rule than to subject everyone in an organization, family or society to such a limiting and crippling leadership approach.

No wonder all the venerable spiritual leaders and texts talk not about empathy, but about compassion (a well-defined word used in English since the early 1300's), because compassion has been universally understood to quickly translate into meaningful decisions that produce action.[109] And decisive and meaningful action infuses rather than depletes energy, creating more of the positive emotional fuel and fulfillment that comes from moving beyond emotions to actually serving others. That's a big win-win vs. the lose-lose that our popular notions of empathy can create.

We can each help counter these unproductive trends and raise the bar for morally decisive leadership by:

• Raising our personal balance of decisive action over rhetoric and emotion, and encouraging others to do likewise.

• Confronting any lack of moral integrity, clarity or courage in decisions long before the casualties start to add up.

- Challenging the cultural chorus of applause for those whose soothing words and expressions of empathy do not align with their decisions and behavior.
- Refusing to become so enamored with popular thought and fads that we lose any intellectual curiosity as to their potential limits and unintended consequences.

Seeing the higher and longer-term moral implications of popular thought and cultural trends is, in my experience, a rarity among leaders and yet a critical distinguishing mark of every leader who makes consistently effective decisions, as it was with Lincoln. Even with regard to emotional intelligence, a core component and precursor to empathy (emotional recognition) has been demonstrated to

We can point the finger of blame all we wish, but in the end we get leadership, and thus leadership decisions, that reflect our culture. In other words, we get the leadership that we deserve.

have a significant downside for those who have "too much" of that ability, including creating additional stress that affects their decision-making effectiveness.[110]

Effective decision-making is an art that requires a healthy soular system as a foundation, along with constant discipline and learning. Neither of these exists without a conscious approach, a checklist if you will, just as a doctor or attorney uses when the stakes are high, and then a review of the case afterward with an eye to learn and improve. Only then will an effective process become such second nature, that when put to the test, we will have both the courage and insight to make a higher and effective leadership decision and take meaningful action in the moment of truth. Effective leaders like Lincoln, Zelensky and Fred Smith make morally courageous decisions and take action, then do their talking as they are marching forward into battle. Which is why they don't have to slow down every few steps and look back over their shoulder to see if anyone is following.

Steps to Reaching Higher Ground

Purpose

> *The more one forgets himself, by giving himself to a cause to serve or another person to love, the more human he is and the more he actualizes himself. What is called self-actualization is not an attainable aim at all, for the simple reason that the more one would strive for it, the more he would miss it. In other words, self-actualization is possible only as a side-effect of self-transcendence."*
> – Viktor Frankl, *Man's Search for Meaning*

Purpose-driven remains a popular topic evidenced by the growing number of books and Chief Purpose Officer positions. As wonderful as purpose-driven is, I'm here to provide a cautionary note that may help someone avoid the unintended consequences that accrue when we become so enamored with any trend that we develop unrealistic expectations for its magic, or fail to understand the foundational requirements for its development. So I wish to discuss briefly the foundational importance of a deep moral purpose for life as a prerequisite to finding real meaning in any human endeavor. I recommend that you read Davin Salvagno's book, *Finding Purpose at Work,* for an inspiring and integrative perspective on how to discover and apply your highest purpose throughout your career.

Claude Monet's Path to Purpose

I used to think my unique life's purpose and gifts would suddenly become clear…that is, right after the next new book, video, neuroscience research, etc. But that breakthrough came instead by following the path of Monet, whose journey began by revisiting scenes from his childhood on the beaches of Normandy. There he became fascinated by his impressions as the dynamics of light and color changed with the weather. We can learn from his journey to discover his unique gifts and purpose by recognizing that:

- Our childhood brain was relatively unpolluted, so reflecting on what interested or moved us in our youth can hold valuable secrets.
- We need a break from the usual noise and clutter to reflect and explore deeply what is unique about us that holds great potential. Nature is a great facilitator, as is exploring and learning in general. Monet had little

interest in the conventional notion of painting inside in a studio, so exploring other options was an essential move in discovering his unique gift.

- The answer is unlikely to come in a sudden flash of insight. Monet began his journey by simply making imperfect strokes that reflected his intuitive impressions of light and color. Feel and intuition to start combined with dedication to perfecting your work as your passion and purpose become clearer. Monet was observed sitting for hours in the cold and snow, wearing multiple coats, just to practice capturing his impressions of snow in the changing light.

> *No one will see or feel the world quite like you; following what interests and moves you deeply is the path to discovering your unique gifts and purpose.*

My Journey

While a member of the FedEx Leadership Institute, I attended a highly experiential leadership course facilitated by Steve Nielsen, a colleague of mine in the Institute. During that course I experienced a strong impression of the power of experiential learning and Steve's unique ability to connect with and influence leaders at a profound and visceral level. It was just an impression, certainly not one that I recognized any life-changing potential in for me at the time, but one that touched me deeply enough that I did not dismiss it. On a blank canvas I began to think about how to integrate an experiential approach to leadership development with the interest in ethics and psychology that I had developed earlier in graduate work.

I had no idea for several years if my initial impression held any potential for meaningful work that would help others. But as I discarded and refined ideas (Monet destroyed several hundred of his works), my initial impression turned into leadership programs that (if you are to believe participants) have been life-changing in their impact. Beyond the client ROI, the personal implications for growth and success for those who have attended are far beyond what I could have imagined when that first impression was formed. But to transform from impression to purpose, as is the case with the vast majority of people, was a process of faith and work over several years.

Jimmy Braddock the boxer (played by Russell Crowe in Cinderella Man) found the purpose that drove him to success only after suffering poverty, numerous defeats and hardships over the years. When asked by a reporter why he thought he could now win, Jimmy replied that it was because he knew what he was fighting for. "What's that, Jimmy?" asked the reporter. "Milk," Jimmy replied, referring to putting food and drink on his family's table. What do you find worth fighting for, no matter how many defeats you suffer in the process? An easy life is seldom a fulfilled life, and for many the key to a compelling purpose may be found in their past struggles, now reflected in a deeper passion and commitment to something far greater than any personal ambitions.

In my journey, it was a challenging childhood with a difficult father that eventually fueled my desire to help others eliminate the moral blind spots and psychological baggage that accrues from such experiences so they could reach their full potential. This not only brought the deep fulfillment that comes from serving others in a meaningful way, but helped me to continually recognize and leave behind the baggage I was carrying from my childhood experiences. Turning pain into purpose is for many the path to healing for both themselves and others.

No organization's purpose, no matter how noble, can fill the void in our souls if we do not have a compelling purpose for our life that transcends ourselves: compelling because it is grounded in moral principles and values that are timeless and universal. Such a purpose can create beautiful harmony between our thoughts, decisions and actions

You must find a deeper purpose for life before you can find real meaning in work.

while infusing everything we do with passion. It can serve as an anchor for our soul, so that we are not tossed about or broken apart by the storms of life, but rather shine a steadfast light of hope to guide those who may be lost in the darkness.

Leadership Implications

Those with a deeper purpose are naturally more passionate, decisive, inspiring and resilient leaders, and of course more effective in creating a true purpose-driven organization. In reviewing the stories of the most exceptional leaders, the recurring themes I found that may be helpful to you within an organizational leadership context are:

1. Rigorously clarify your purpose, which requires simplification and avoiding the "change the world" overly expansive and thus meaningless scope.[111]

2. Focus on the special value and service you bring to your markets lest your organization's purpose gets confusing and lost from being spread across too many constituents.[112] Beware the risk of becoming politically oriented in your purpose or organization, the unintended consequences of which have abounded in recent years.[113]

Nothing will contribute to your professional growth and success, or your personal fulfillment and joy, more than discovering a deep purpose for your life, even if you have to rediscover the world around you to find it. As long as you keep your purpose grounded in universal moral values, as well as in the story of your life,[114] it will play a profound role in expanding and deepening your ability to influence others. What moves you to great joy or sorrow, to righteous indignation, to immediate action, and makes time fly? These are the windows through which you can begin to see your deep purpose more clearly.

> *"If a man has not discovered something that he will die for, in a sense he is not fit to live."*
> — **Martin Luther King Jr.**

Humility

My favorite definition of humility is that of C. S. Lewis, who defines it not as thinking less of oneself, but as self-forgetfulness, or thinking about our "self" less. Thinking about ourselves less, however, requires that we do not think of ourselves more highly than we should, but that we think of ourselves "soberly" (Romans 12:3). The Greek word for soberly (*sophroneo*) means to think realistically, or as aligns with reality, neither higher nor lower. There are key reasons why this reality-based perspective is such an important part of genuine humility and effective moral leadership:

1. Trying to maintain inflated notions of ourselves as some special guru or enlightened soul is not only a full-time, but futile endeavor, because our moral conscience doesn't buy fiction, only reality. Thus, the first critical step to avoid being afflicted with imposter syndrome is not to be an imposter.

2. Accepting that we are all flawed works in progress allows us to relax and focus on learning, growth and contribution rather than suffer the great stress of continually trying to prop up inflated notions of ourselves. Even Einstein said, "I have no special talents, I am only passionately curious." No wonder his brain was so agile, as he was free of the stress we experience when we struggle against our higher moral voice to inflate our importance or capabilities. Bejamin Franklin articulated

his insights on humility, communication and learning after reading an account of the trial of Socrates:

"I continu'd this method some few years, but gradually left it, retaining only the habit of expressing myself in terms of modest diffidence; never using, when I advanced anything that may possibly be disputed, the words certainly, undoubtedly, or any others that give the air of positiveness to an opinion; but rather say, I conceive or apprehend a thing to be so and so; it appears to me, or I should think it so or so, for such and such reasons; or I imagine it to be so; or it is so, if I am not mistaken. This habit, I believe, has been of great advantage to me when I have had occasion to inculcate my opinions, and persuade men into measures that I have been from time to time engaged in promoting; and, as the chief ends of conversation are to inform or to be informed, to please or to persuade, I wish well-meaning, sensible men would not lessen their power of doing good by a positive, assuming manner, that seldom fails to disgust, tends to create opposition, and to defeat everyone of those purposes for which speech was given to us, to wit, giving or receiving information or pleasure. For, if you would inform, a positive and dogmatical manner in advancing your sentiments may provoke contradiction and prevent a candid attention. If you wish information and improvement from the knowledge of others, and yet at the same time express yourself as firmly fix'd in your present opinions, modest, sensible men, who do not love disputation,

will probably leave you undisturbed in the possession of your error. And by such a manner, you can seldom hope to recommend yourself in pleasing your hearers, or to persuade those whose concurrence you desire."[15]

3. People trust, respect and can relate to a leader who has a realistic self-image; no one can trust a leader with self-delusions because they are continually creating collateral damage with their misplaced hubris. People trust and admire humble leaders because they readily accept blame, eagerly give credit, admit mistakes and apologize when needed.

4. Having a realistic perspective helps us to avoid defrauding others by overpromising and underdelivering. This admittedly flies in the face of popular advice that tells us that we can do anything, that everyone is a genius, and that if asked to do something we don't know how to do, just say yes and then figure it out later. I frankly don't want to be on the receiving end of the product or service that someone is trying to figure out on the fly. Nothing will deflate our self-esteem and confidence more quickly than such notions that do not account for reality.

Having a realistic view of ourselves, paradoxically, also enables us to capture our highest potential, because then we work to improve ourselves based on the reality of our true gifts, strengths and weaknesses. Someone with a delusional view of themselves cannot improve in reality, because reality is not their starting point. Thus humility is the secret to building the only self-esteem that is healthy and sustainable, because real confidence comes only from real learning, growth, influence and impact, not from wishful thinking or self-talk.

Lincoln illustrated the power and benefits of these four reasons to be realistically humble through his habit of consistently declaring "that he, and not his Cabinet, was in fault for errors imputed to them."[116] He went so far in defending Secretary of War Stanton after he was accused of failing to send sufficient troops to the Peninsula Campaign (Virginia) that he called for a major rally at the Capitol on his behalf. Speaking at the rally Lincoln proclaimed that he believed Stanton to be a "brave and able man, and I stand here, as justice requires me to do, to take upon myself what has been charged on the Secretary of War."[117]

The power of Lincoln's humility is clearly evident in the transformation in his relationship with Stanton, because despite the fact that "no two men were ever more utterly and irreconcilably unlike" (according to Stanton's secretary), and despite his earlier harsh dismissals of Lincoln as a political leader, at the end "Stanton not only revered Lincoln; he loved him."[118] In a culture bemoaning the lack of accountability, loyalty and discretionary effort, while blaming others first and foremost for these deficits, it would be hard to overstate the value of reflecting upon the full implications of Lincoln's example.

This is one of many examples of such humility you will find should you read more about Lincoln in the fine works available.

Rather than demand accountability and loyalty, he prioritized holding himself accountable and demonstrating loyalty to others, understanding that his example would prompt far higher levels of these traits than his rhetoric about how important they were. He also understood that holding yourself accountable first and foremost was the key to learning and growing in your leadership capabilities faster than anyone expected.

The roots of this humility can be traced back to his failure to keep his promises to the people of Illinois and to Mary Todd, after which he devoted himself to such a realistic and sober self-assessment that he concluded that he could no longer trust himself in any matter of much importance. He admitted his weakness in finance and his role in the recession to the citizens of Illinois, and after returning to legal practice said candidly, "I am not an accomplished lawyer."[119] Noteworthy at any age, this humble self-evaluation and the subsequent years of renewed devotion to impeccable integrity, learning and growth at the age of forty is quite remarkable.

Lincoln could have exercised his rational voice and quite easily blamed the financial debacle in Illinois on a great number of other people and factors. He could have allowed his emotional voice to use the stress in his relationship with Mary Todd to forever justify ending their relationship and breaking his promise. Instead, he chose to focus on the only variable in these scenarios over which he had full control, himself. As well stated by Doris Kearns Goodwin, "To fulfill what he believed to be his destiny, a different kind of sustained effort and discipline was required, a willingness to confront weakness and imperfection, reflect upon failure, and examine the kind of leader he wanted to be."[120]

The humility that produced this relentless self-examination and constant learning was still evident over fifteen years later, and just days before his death, when President Lincoln walked away from three thousand supporters clamoring for him to make a Civil War victory speech at the White House. While Lincoln wisely took the opportunity to prioritize the theme of uniting the nation by asking the Marine band to play Dixie, he also stated that he needed additional time to think further on what he should say. How many times have you declined to share your opinion or ideas because you recognized the need to contemplate more deeply and prepare more carefully? Decisions like these help us truly evaluate ourselves by the Lincoln standard and to understand why so many fall so far short of his integrity and influence.

The best way I know to develop and maintain this humble reality-based view of ourselves is to get candid feedback from those who live in the reality that we create through our decisions and behavior. Asking for feedback in writing is a good first step if you do not have the comfort to do so in person, but relationships where people care enough to be candid are critical to long-term growth. To provoke further thought in this area, and as a prompt for good questions to ask, I suggest reading Peter Drucker's classic article on *Managing Oneself*.[121] And, as he suggests, each time you make a decision, write down the impact you expect to see in the future. Then, at the appropriate later time, write down what you perceive the impact to have been, and then ask those you trust to give you their perspective. This will provide you with invaluable learning and the insight required to not only have a more realistic view of yourself, but to identify major growth opportunities for greater moral clarity and courage in decisions as well.

A Function of Purpose

Humility, from my perspective, is the natural result of finding a higher purpose for one's life, just as emotional health and intelligence is the natural output of a healthy soular system. In fact, most of the leadership attributes we recognize as critical to building trust and influence are the natural outputs of a highly integrated soular system led by our moral voice, along with a clear and deep purpose that defines the path along which we invest ourselves. For example, a servant leadership orientation is just the natural byproduct of our higher moral voice leading a healthy soular system. So while I have read many helpful books and research papers on servant leadership, the natural path to becoming more service oriented is to strengthen the inner leadership role of our self-transcendent moral voice, and then clearly define the purpose and focus of our service in a compelling way that fuels positive emotional energy.

The more we define and deepen the moral clarity of our purpose, and the more clearly we perceive the great need in the world for our gifts, the more we will recognize our inability and limitations to serve that need fully. And the more we learn about our chosen area of purpose, the more we will recognize how much larger the universe of potential knowledge that we do not possess. It is impossible to think unrealistically or too highly of ourselves with this perspective, informed by our limitations to meet the world's great needs and aware of the vast universe of knowledge beyond our ability to master. Driven by such a perspective we will naturally seek feedback to improve, ask for help, listen with an ear to learn, and remain focused on the big picture over the long-term rather than on ourselves in the moment.

Lincoln provides a compelling example of the nature and power of humility when driven by a higher moral purpose. When Lincoln appointed his three bitter political rivals to the top three positions on his Cabinet, it was because he deemed these three men instrumental to his purpose of saving the Union.[122] Further, he was keenly aware of his lack of experience in the politically charged halls of Washington at a moment in history when such a limitation could preclude him from ever realizing this noble purpose. This keen awareness of his limitations and weaknesses enabled him to draw from a wide variety of leaders with compensating strengths and political experience for his entire Cabinet.

This reality-based assessment of himself demonstrates the genuine humility missing in many leaders, who in his position would have thought rather highly of themselves at being elected President of the United States. Such leaders would have been driven by their emotional or rational dimensions to make completely different Cabinet decisions, excluding all of these bitter political enemies, and doing so with clear and compelling justifications in the eyes of most people. As with his decision to play Dixie rather than make a victory speech when Lee surrendered, however, Lincoln's humility, informed by the deep purpose of saving a nation, shows how counter to conventional wisdom moral leadership often appears at first glance.

President Lincoln had the humility, moral clarity and leadership insights that came from a much longer and higher view of the battlefield than those who are so wrapped up in themselves that they can't see past their ego, and thus seek the comfort of safe spaces and echo chambers where head nods in agreement every time they speak. Leaders with humility understand that they can improve only as fast as they learn, and that they learn nothing by listening to themselves talk or to the soothing tones of those who second their every motion.

And there is no question as to the wisdom and impact of Lincoln's atypical decision from the longer lens of history. His wisdom in choosing this cabinet is evidenced not only by their decisions that saved the Union, but by how loyal and devoted these former rivals became to the President. Seward, for example, often said publicly that Lincoln was the best and wisest man he had ever known and for weeks after the President's death Seward was inconsolable, often breaking into tears suddenly, even in public. Such a deep, rewarding, productive and enduring relationship is only possible with someone with the humility and self-transcendent purpose of Lincoln.

Humility, Self-Esteem and Self-Respect

While writing this book I came across a post from a coach offering to teach me how to develop the confidence to believe that I "deserve the world and can do anything." It seems there are an increasing number of people either coaching leaders on self-esteem and confidence or working on it daily. Which begs the question, if the popular cure so heavily promoted for decades now is so effective, why does the disease not only persist, but seem to be increasing?

The self-esteem movement has been all the rage since the 1960's, with a variety of readings and programs designed to enhance self-esteem beginning at the earliest ages of childhood. For a detailed review of the enormous scale of this movement and its failures I suggest you read *The Quick Fix: Why Fad Psychology Can't Cure Our Social Ills* by Jesse Singal, or review some of the scholarly research illustrating its broken promises and unintended consequences.[123] And then explore recent research on the upside of what is now labeled imposter syndrome,[124] once understood to be a normal human condition called humility with significant personal and career benefits. Of course I am not addressing those who truly suffer from an unrealistic and debilitating lack of self-esteem, but within the leadership population greater humility, not less, is the key to balancing other leadership traits to ensure positive influence and relationships.[125]

That we are a culture out of balance as a result of this decades-long "self" obsession is evident in the significant change of frequency with which the words self-esteem and humility have occurred in literature.

Changes in Usage Frequency of "Self-esteem"

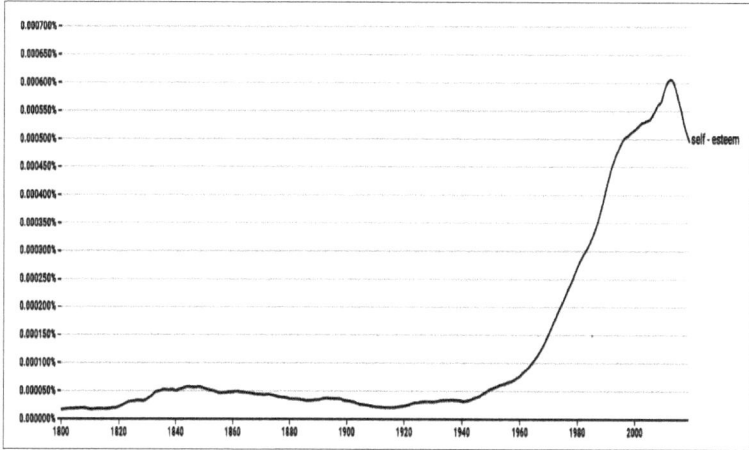

Changes in Usage Frequency of "Humility"

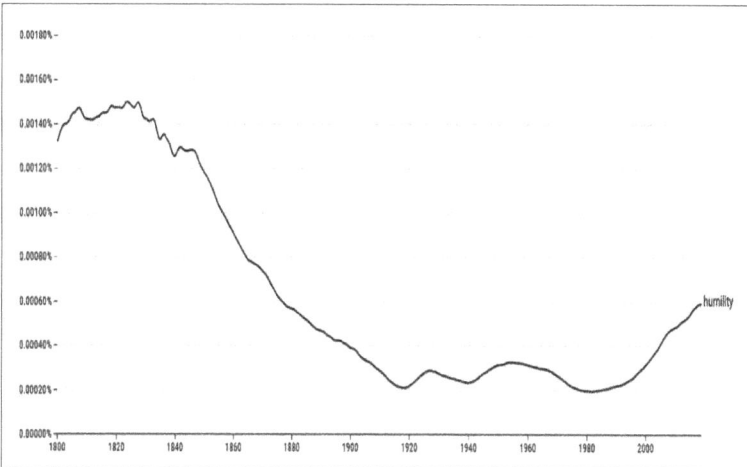

This trend is rooted in the macro cultural shift discussed earlier that elevates self, self-expression, or anything self-related above the perspective that recognizes not only the existence of universal moral values, but the importance of humbling one's "self" in service to those values in order to build and preserve civil, functional and healthy organizations and societies. To anyone working to develop themselves or others as a moral leader, an understanding of the depth and implications of this shift is of great importance. The bottom line is that we must build self-respect by conforming to universal moral values before we can feel any deep and sustainable self-esteem. In other words, we must earn it.

> *Chasing self-esteem is futile because self-esteem is the natural by-product of self-respect.*

Fueled by Gratitude

In stark contrast to this cultural shift I give you Rip Wheeler from the Yellowstone TV series. Some of you will recall the advice he gave to a homeless and troubled young teen on how to achieve success in this world. While most self-esteem experts would have worked to inflate his self-image, Rip gave the kid a job cleaning out horse stables, along with his secret to success: *Don't ever think you deserve it.*

This rare counter-culture attitude prompts us to be grateful for whatever we have, including for just waking up each morning, and then for many little things that others take for granted. Such gratitude takes our focus off our "self," so that we do not become so self-absorbed that we spend most of our life all tangled up and trapped within ourselves. This larger perspective enables us to see and capitalize on the beauty and opportunities others who can't see beyond themselves inevitably miss. It also helps us better understand how to leverage our unique gifts as we become more aware of the world around us.

Rip was onto something according to a review of the leading research on gratitude by Harvard Medical School that found it has significant benefits to our mental and emotional health, as well as to our general happiness.[126] Could it be another life and leadership paradox that the humility to think that we deserve nothing is one of the most liberating and empowering attitudes we can have? A great weight lifted from our souls that frees us to experience daily gratitude and the joy of finding a higher and larger purpose beyond our self? Of course, as always, I may be wrong...but Rip Wheeler?

Humility or Emotional Intelligence?

Popular articles about Patrick Mahomes, the quarterback who led the Kansas City Chiefs to a Super Bowl victory, provide an interesting case study in how the fundamental importance of humility to leadership effectiveness has been lost in the cultural shift discussed earlier, a shift that has led to a preoccupation with self-expression and emotional intelligence. One article at Inc., among many you can easily find, credits Mahomes with a masterclass in emotional intelligence because he declined to say he was the "face of the NFL" after the Super Bowl victory. Instead, he credited other legends with that honor. This Inc. article and others credit Mahomes' exceptional success, leadership ability, performance under pressure (coming from behind to win every playoff game), remarkable recovery after throwing two interceptions and even post-victory priorities to his emotional intelligence.[127]

What was striking to me, and totally neglected in these articles, is that just a few days earlier in an interview Mahomes described how his deep faith in God, faith that places himself and football in proper perspective, is responsible for his success,[128] stating that his primary goal on the field is to glorify God. One would think that business writers who credit Mahomes with such a high level of self-awareness would lend credibility to his own words, but alas, that is the power of culturally driven bias. As previously noted, Lincoln's decision to staff his cabinet with political rivals has been often attributed to emotional intelligence, while his own words that clearly ground his decision in humility and a servant perspective are equally neglected.

Patrick Mahomes' exceptional leadership, resilience and performance under immense pressure is just another compelling example of the power of humility and a servant leadership perspective. When you are not enamored with and focused on yourself and your statistics, then you do not become emotionally frustrated with the mistakes you have just made. You can quickly move beyond them because you have lost your "self" in a much bigger picture. You learn much faster because you are not sensitive to or easily offended by constructive feedback, rather you view it as an opportunity to better advance a larger purpose and mission. Patrick Mahomes doesn't credit emotional intelligence for his leadership success or performance under pressure because his emotional health and resilience is the natural product of his fundamental perspective on himself, his life and his profession.

Of course there is always work to do to better understand and manage our emotions, and a wealth of good literature available to help us do that. But exceptional emotional health and resilience comes only to those who recognize that humility and a higher moral perspective are required to proactively create emotional health, while those focused on the end of process emotions, rather than the root causes, are continually trapped in a reactive management and corrective mode. Whether it is to better understand how our cultural shift has diminished and obscured the importance of this root cause foundation, or how humility and servant leadership are inextricably linked,[129] I would encourage you to continue to explore this subject to help both yourself and others on their leadership development journey.

Forgiveness

During my favorite episode of the old TV Western Gunsmoke, Trafton (Victor French) shoots a priest during a robbery. The last act of the priest before dying is to make the sign of the cross on Trafton's forehead with his bloodstained hands as he speaks his last words, "I forgive." After the priest forgives him Trafton is a changed man. He begins seeking out those he has hurt in the past, trying to make amends and asking for forgiveness, but no one has any interest in forgiving him. They all, of course, are well justified with plenty of emotionally or rationally driven reasons for withholding their mercy. Finding no forgiveness, he confronts Marshall Matt Dillon in a scene where he knows the Marshall will shoot and kill him. Better to die, he decides, than to live unforgiven. His last words to Marshall Dillon as he is dying? "I forgive."

When we refuse to forgive it's usually about us. No matter how much we have been wronged, we are often guilty of doing something we knew to be wrong in the process as well. We twist and turn our own guilt into resentment and bitterness toward the other person in a futile effort to rationalize that for which there is no justification. As Nelson Mandela said, this is like drinking poison and expecting it to kill the other person. Dying may in fact be a better alternative to this slow death of our soul.

Rembrandt was so enamored with the subject of forgiveness that he painted the return of the prodigal son (a parable told by Jesus) at least three times, the most famous of these painted just two years before his death. I think of this parable by Jesus as a story more about a forgiving father than one about a prodigal son, as it has come to be known. The father's behavior is exceptional, the son's is routine. After all, the son had taken his father's inheritance early and then wasted it all in a foreign land before he came to his senses and returned home begging for forgiveness. In other words, it was his last option.

The father on the other hand forgives his son despite having many reasons not to after being so forsaken and disrespected. Like the older brother, he could have easily folded his hands in judgment and withheld forgiveness and restoration, articulating a long list of reasons justifying his decision. Which one do we most resemble?

Lincoln reflected this father's spirit of forgiveness consistently, as in when he appointed Edward Staton as his Secretary of War, despite the fact that Staton had publicly humiliated Lincoln in the famous Reaper Case only seven years earlier. Reviewing how rude and dismissive Stanton was in his treatment of Lincoln,[130] it is worthwhile reflecting on how willing we would be to forgive such behavior, much less appoint that person to a senior leadership role. But in Lincoln's case, "If a man had maligned him, or been guilty of personal ill-treatment or abuse, and was the fittest man for the place, he would put them in his Cabinet just as soon as he would his friend."[131]

Forgiveness holds such healing and redemptive power precisely because it elevates us to a spiritual plane far above any human rhyme or reason. As such, it is the one act where we humans, though earthbound for a time, may reach out and touch the heart of God. So before we speak our last words, perhaps we should think about whom we have yet to forgive… or ask to forgive us…and why.

Moral Exercise and Leverage

As mentioned, I remember the first time I heard Fred Smith speak with great clarity, although it was decades ago. In that speech to young managers he emphasized the importance of what is often called the Pareto principle, generally described as the phenomenon that about 80% of any outcomes are produced by around 20% of the inputs or causes. He stressed the importance of identifying and focusing our managerial energy on that 20%, because trying to get everything on our desk finished on any day was (at least at FedEx) a truly impossible task. When you do that you soon find yourself ahead of the learning curve, eliminating root causes to problems and advancing your management skills at a surprising rate.

Becoming a stronger moral leader follows the same principle, as we all have what can easily seem like an overwhelming amount of moral work to do. Since we are never going to arrive at perfection, the best we can do is select an area with high leverage for us because of its inordinate return on our investment of attention and energy. That ROI may be found where there is an immediate and urgent need to improve relationships, as well as in what we perceive as smaller infractions that occur frequently, and thus give us more opportunities to exercise and strengthen our higher moral dimension. Those opportunities are easy for most of us to find in untrue statements like "tell them I'm not in," or in the daily words we speak to appease others or advance ourselves that are neither true nor sincere. As Jordan Peterson advises in *12 Rules for*

Life, this one exercise alone is unnerving, but an important early step to strengthening our moral voice so that it has the gravitational pull of an exceptional leader like Lincoln.

If you have completed the reflection exercises in this book, you should have developed insights into any unconscious leadership roles your rational or emotional voices are playing in your soular system. Those insights exercise and expand your moral clarity daily, if you apply them daily. To apply them, however, requires a willingness to pause the mile-a-minute autopilot many leaders operate on and to ask yourself a silent Golden Rule or integrity question at the appropriate time. As your moral clarity increases from this silent process the question and answer will eventually occur unconsciously in real time, and though it may feel like a ten-second pause initially to you, all anyone else will notice is that perhaps you are taking a second to be thoughtful and intentional. Perhaps not a bad thing for one to notice about a leader? And the great news is that each day this process becomes more natural and unconscious until like Lincoln, no matter the nature or urgency of the challenge, we can intuitively make the right leadership call on the spot.

Unconscious Freedom or Prison?

The risk of not intentionally exercising our moral voice is that we become unconsciously competent at lower moral behavior, which clearly seems to be the default path over the course of human history. In some dramatic scenarios in the news this default state is crystalized, as in an incident aboard the

Washington D.C. area Red Line Metro train on the Saturday afternoon of July 4, 2015. An eighteen-year-old man, who was 5' 5" tall and who weighed only 125 pounds, killed a recent college graduate, Kevin Sutherland, after Sutherland resisted the attempt to rob him of his mobile phone. While numerous witnesses watched but did nothing to intervene, the robber stabbed Sutherland thirty to forty times, then proceeded to rob others on the train until it stopped, where he exited without any attempt to stop him.

It is instructive to hear the reasons several witnesses gave for not attempting to stop the killing in a scenario where the perpetrator was so small and clearly outnumbered.[132] One person was clearly emotionally driven as they stated that their instinct was to "stay put and try to become as small as possible." Another gave the man extra money from their pocket after their wallet was taken in a rational calculation to keep the robber from hurting their father. Another stated they weren't sure what they needed to do. Several of those who stood by doing nothing admitted they were talking among themselves while Sutherland was being repeatedly stabbed, saying it was too dangerous to try and stop the killing, and even telling those who looked ready to do something, "Don't do that." One even admitted to the cold rational calculation of "I wanted him to think that he could walk away from this, and that's what he did."

It doesn't take much thought to see how these same decisions and behaviors, driven by our rational and emotional voices, occur in everyday personal and organizational scenarios. Does "stay put and try to become as small as possible" look familiar? Or trying to calculate how to get on the good side of a corrupt leader so you will be spared? Or dissuading others from doing the right thing because it's too dangerous? Or just hoping to be the one person who walks away unharmed? Just as Kevin Sutherland's life could have, and should have been saved, there are countless casualties in organizational life that can be saved through moral leadership. Todd Farchoine, a clinical psychologist and Professor at Boston University who was interviewed by CBS news after the incident, said that if only one person on the train would have taken the lead in trying to stop Sutherland's murder, others would have immediately stepped in also. "When somebody does step in, others will as well."

In other words, everyone knows what the right thing to do is, but because they have spent their life exercising their emotional or rational dimension more than their moral voice, these loudest and strongest inner voices will drive their behavior in any coin toss or moment of truth decision. To think that our moral voice will lead us in important decisions, when we have subordinated it to our rational or emotional voice for years, is as futile as training for the Olympic marathon but then entering the weightlifting competition. But since the Golden Rule is a universal value embedded deep within the human heart, even those with a diminished moral voice will step up to the plate and do the right thing more often than not if a moral leader will set the example. When everyone is looking around for someone else to exhibit the moral clarity and courage to do the right thing, that is when a moral leader saves the day because of the years they have spent exercising their moral voice in so many mundane and ostensibly insignificant scenarios.

At the other end of the moral spectrum are people like Harry Gregg, the goalkeeper for Manchester United, who was onboard the horrific crash in February, 1958 of the aircraft carrying the team back from Belgrade. Their aircraft failed to clear the snow-covered runway during takeoff after a refueling stop in Munich, crashing and bursting into flames, killing 23 of the 40 passengers and seriously injuring many others. Harry heard the pilot shouting "Run, it's going to explode!" with those instructions followed by all who heard them with the exception of Harry Gregg. Harry ran back inside the burning aircraft 3 times to pull out passengers trapped inside, including the pregnant wife of a Yugoslav diplomat and her young daughter, and five of his teammates, the last two of whom were unconscious. Eight other Manchester United players perished in the crash.

In interviews over the years about his heroic action, Harry dismissed any attempts to elevate him as a hero, saying only "I did what had to be done," and then in his last interview before his death saying, "I never considered myself to be John Wayne or a hero or anything. I just did things that came naturally."[133] It is striking to me that in the train murder scenario, in the Manchester United crash, and in many other similar scenarios

I found exactly the same language used by those who were morally courageous and heroic and by those who were not. Some of those who stood silently by while Kevin Sutherland was murdered in later interviews spoke of "having no choice," and then cited their justifications, mainly concern for their own safety. Meanwhile, in numerous stories of moral heroics where people risked their lives to save others precisely the same language is used. They didn't have time to think about their decision, they had no choice, like Harry Greg they just did what had to be done, they did what came naturally.

Despite the similarity in language, unsurprising given that our soular system output under stress will be no better or worse than the input we have provided over the years, there is still a striking difference that remains after the words. Those who did the right thing enjoy lasting inner peace knowing that they were true to the deepest universal moral values we all share. Those who acted otherwise, however, are forever trapped in a prison of their own construction, because their conscience will demand justification for their lack of moral clarity and courage, and yet even their most carefully constructed rationalizations will be deemed inadequate. Thus they will relive their decisions countless times, perhaps eventually unconsciously, but still no less disruptive to the inner peace we all seek.

While leaders may never face a life or death scenario like Harry Gregg, any leader will make decisions with significant, and often life-changing implications for others and for their organization. And it is only through the daily discipline of consciously exercising our moral voice in every scenario that moral clarity and courage eventually come naturally to us. To reach this point of freedom, where we know and do the right thing unconsciously, brings not only an inner peace that no outside person or force can disrupt, but an almost omnipotent power like Lincoln's to influence even those who are reluctant bystanders to stand up and join the fight for what is right.

Moral Courage Is Built Through Moral Exercise

"I learned that courage was not the absence of fear, but the triumph over it. The brave man is not he who does not feel afraid, but he who conquers that fear."
— **Nelson Mandela**

"Fear is a reaction. Courage is a decision."
— **Winston Churchill**

As I searched beyond citizens like Harry Gregg for well-known modern leaders with whom writers associated the words courage and integrity,[134] Nelson Mandela's and Margaret Thatcher's names came up more often than any others.[135] And the more I learned about Thatcher, the more I understood why she was the first British Prime Minister to be elected to three full terms. Her father was a grocer, and as a woman from a modest family, it was absurd to think she could ever be a leader in the chambers of British government, long renowned for chauvinism and class distinctions. But through her youth and academic years at Oxford she had proven herself uncompromising in her devotion to integrity and high moral values, which led to her appointment as the first woman President of the Oxford University Conservative Association.

When she became the first woman Prime Minister of Britain in 1979 she inherited a depressed economy, disastrous monetary policies and skyrocketing interest rates. Undeterred by political opponents, she had the courage to make what she viewed as necessary decisions to keep Britain from collapsing into an economic catastrophe for all its citizens. Her courage would play a major role not only in the restoration of a strong Britain, but also in the collapse of the Soviet Union and the end of the Cold War.

Even Meryl Streep, quite a distance removed from Thatcher's political positions, wrote a tribute to her leadership and to the personal integrity and courage that enabled her to remain true to her convictions, in spite of what Streep characterized as "unprecedented" hatred from those in the opposing party.[136] Streep concluded by noting a wonderful benefit of Thatcher's courage, "to have given women and girls around the world reason to supplant fantasies of being princesses with a different dream: the real-life option of leading their nation; this was groundbreaking and admirable."

Such was her courage under duress that I even found articles from this year wishing for leaders to tackle current economic challenges with the clarity, courage and decisiveness of Thatcher, rather than shifting responsibility or bemoaning the lack of solutions as seems to be the norm. To give you an idea of just how impeccable her integrity was let me share this excerpt from *There is No Alternative: Why Margaret Thatcher Matters* by Claire Berlinski:

> "Lady Thatcher was under no obligation to give her personal papers to anyone. Indeed, she could have sold them to the highest bidder or burnt them had she thought it prudent. She instead donated them to the British people. This is proof of the depth of her commitment to the ideal of an open society, not to mention an extraordinary testimony to her confidence in her own character. You do not hand over to historians and journalists 3,000 boxes of papers, many of which you have not seen since the day they crossed your desk, if you are not certain that you have always conducted yourself with irreproachable integrity. Think about it: Would you?"

From whence comes such moral clarity, consistency and courage? It comes from seeing the moral dimension in every decision, as did Lincoln, and in exercising your moral voice until your rational and emotional dimensions are naturally subordinate and executing effectively their designed and healthy supporting roles. I have no interest in evaluating her political positions or policies, which obviously had some significant benefits in the critical situation she entered, and some limitations and unfavorable consequences as well, as could be said of most any politician. But the incredible moral courage it took to remain true to her values was a key to her ability to bring economic stability to Britain against such strong resistance and relentless personal attacks.

The point I hope to reinforce here is that long before Thatcher encountered the storm through which she led Britain, and the Cold War that she played no small role in ending, she was daily exercising moral insight and courage in decisions and scenarios that appeared to have absolutely no significance in the moment. Nor did she abandon that practice when she became Prime Minister, in fact it would have been nearly impossible for her to have done so, because by then it was natural and unconscious behavior, just as it was with Lincoln.[137] In fact, Lord Conrad Black, who knew her well and interacted with her often said, "Margaret Thatcher was very courageous and very admirable, also a wonderful person in small ways. The staff at Downing Street and Chequers loved her: she was terribly polite to these people."[138] During this conversation with Jordan Peterson, Black describes and contrasts how respectfully and courteously Thatcher treated, for example, someone who was serving tea, with how those politicians who attacked her and claimed to be the true advocates for ordinary men and women treated others.

Thatcher, Mandela and Lincoln recognized what so few aspiring or current leaders understand. They knew that they were "putting it up" their whole life, i.e. that in all the moments, decisions and interactions deemed insignificant by most, they were in fact exercising and strengthening the character traits and courage that would inevitably be revealed in all their big decisive moments. Because as previously stated in the coin toss story, the character we have built over the years is the only one there to be called upon when the decisions become life altering for us or others.

And even if you combine personal and professional decisions, there are likely to only be a handful of really significant decisions made over the course of an entire lifetime. So with no chance to repeatedly practice for those moments of truth, major decisions do not build character as much as they reveal the character we have built in all those countless smaller moments that preceded them. Just as the strength of guilt signals from our amygdala decreases with every small lie, the exercise of moral will to do the right thing with every person, in every scenario, will likewise reduce the strength of emotional fear signals and increase our moral courage in future situations.

> *"Plan for what is difficult while it is easy,*
> *do what is great while it is small."*
> — Sun Tzu, *The Art of War*

Courage is thus a character trait that can only be developed and strengthened through exercise, a trait that reflects the strength of our moral will to overcome any shorter term rational or emotional considerations and do what is right in the face of risk and uncertainty. It was thus considered by Aristotle to be the virtue of first importance since it is a prerequisite to acting upon our higher moral voice rather than succumbing to other forces or considerations. It was, however, to Aristotle a virtue defined more carefully and narrowly, integrating both the healthy fear and confidence required to produce choices that are morally right.[139] A leader with the longer view from the moral high ground sees and feels both the pain that can be inflicted from bad decisions, as well as the higher pleasure that good decisions eventually bring to all. Thus an appreciation of their relative value, and the moral insight to draw from both fear and confidence is essential to moral courage in our decisions and actions.

Nelson Mandela provides what may be the most compelling example of how moral courage is developed by exercising moral insight and discipline in everyday scenarios, including those in which most people fail to see even the slightest moral implications, much less the lasting pain or pleasure that Mandela had the vision to see. Of his twenty-seven years in prison, eighteen of those were spent on Robben Island in a small cell with the floor as his bed. He was allowed one visitor each year for only thirty minutes and could write and receive only one letter every six months. The rest of his time was spent primarily in hard labor in the island's quarry, crushing and carrying rocks at a pace designed to torture the body and break the spirit. It should be a matter of great curiosity as to how the militant and defiant man who entered prison managed to become trusted with the leadership of his fellow prisoners, win the goodwill and trust of the most hardened prison guards and officials and emerge a leader with the moral character and courage to bring disparate factions together and forge the new democratic nation of South Africa.

Of all that has been written, the most instructive insights I gained into Mandela's transformation came from reading the accounts of those who were sent to Robben Island after Mandela, who expected to meet in prison the same militant person they knew prior to his imprisonment. Neville Alexander was a young revolutionary who was sent to Robben Island shortly after Mandela, arriving with the expectation of doing everything possible to fight the unjust oppression and conditions. Shortly after his arrival, however, Mandela confronted Alexander and other younger militants with a stark choice. Either they could act in ways to ensure harsher conditions and punishments, or they could chose to actually learn something from the experience.[140] One of the younger revolutionaries, Strini Moodley, had a cell that was directly across from Mandela. He describes how the younger prisoners had an aggressive attitude toward the warden and guards, refusing "to treat them as though they deserved to be treated as human beings."[141]

As time passed and these younger militants talked more with Mandela and observed what Moodley described as his "conciliatory approach" with the warden and guards, an approach that reflected the Golden Rule, the younger prisoners began to appreciate the radically different relationship dynamics and results from Mandela's approach. Due to his leadership they eventually determined to become "model prisoners" and to treat the guards as they would wish to be treated, rather than as less than human. Many of the onerous burdens and restrictions of prison life were lifted over time as this Golden Rule stimulus and example of moral leadership produced its inevitable response. Most notable and compelling among many examples was the complete transformation over the years of a guard named Kalloman, whom Alexander described initially as a "real brute." Kalloman eventually was so affected by Mandela's behavior that he came to treat Mandela "not just like a gentleman, but really like someone who was not a prisoner."

After de Klerk released Mandela from prison and he was elected the President of South Africa in 1994, his behavior stands in stark contrast to leaders who think such an appointment elevates them above others to a position of power rather than to one of service. His great humility and practice of the Golden Rule,[142] even to a gardener he was simply passing by,[143] was the reason why he so quickly gained the trust of those of every race and even former enemies to achieve breakthroughs that those with the typical approach to leadership could not approach in unlimited lifetimes. It is no accident that those with the most profound leadership accomplishments and moral courage in history

If knowledge of the right thing to do produced moral courage, we would have heaven on earth. Moral courage is built only through the discipline of daily moral exercise.

shared the same habit of daily exercising their highest moral voice, without exception, in every situation, with every single person, no matter their status, over the course of many years.

The man in the photo with Mandela is Christo Brand, who as a lad of only 19 came to serve as a guard at the infamous prison on Robben Island. But a decade of guarding Nelson Mandela transformed his life, and Brand broke many rules as he came to trust and respect Mandela, smuggling food and letters for him and allowing him to hold his infant grandson. The guards eventually came to respect and trust Mandela so much that they consistently sought his advice on how to modify the rules to make prison life better.

Why this miraculous transformation? Because Mandela devoted himself to practicing the Golden Rule by treating even the harshest guards as he would wish to be treated. If you want to change the response, change the stimulus, i.e., yourself. Thirty years after he arrived as a guard Christo Brand returned to the World Heritage Museum on Robben Island to work with 8 former guards and 20 former prisoners to honor Mandela's legacy of leadership. Nelson Mandela finally realized his dream of changing the world when he stopped trying to change the world and began changing himself.

As with Lincoln's ability to see the long-term moral implications in every decision and action, courageous leaders like Thatcher and Mandela, leaders who moved the needle of human history through their moral courage and resilience, developed this leadership trait through the daily exercise of habits that would be foreign to many and even deemed foolish and counterproductive by others. But only those who understand the power of daily exercising the Golden Rule and impeccable integrity in every scenario can ever build the moral clarity and courage required in moments of great challenge to save their team, organization, or perhaps if called upon, even a nation.

CHAPTER 11

Out of the Ashes

*"When we are no longer able to change a situation,
we are challenged to change ourselves."*
—Victor Frankl, *Man's Search for Meaning*

Moral Leadership and Change

Murray Lowe, an Australian photographer, set out in 2020 to document how the unprecedented bush-fires had devastated the area near his home on the coast of New South Wales. What he found amazed him and can be an invaluable lesson for us. He found life and hope in the form of beautiful flowers springing from the ashes only three weeks after the fires.[144] On the face of it, that is more than just unlikely, it's a miracle.

Yet these principles that have been at work since time began can help us discover the "simplicity beyond complexity" that Oliver Wendell Holmes Jr. said he would give his all to

239

discover. These natural systems follow the life-cycle phases of forming, growth and transformation to produce a butterfly from a lowly caterpillar, as well as rare, expensive and incredibly hard diamonds from common graphite so soft and cheap it is the basis for a No. 2 pencil. Humans have captured the lessons from these transformational processes to produce the silicon-based chip at the heart of your PC from sand, the laser that has revolutionized science and healthcare from everyday light, and the carbon fiber composites used in aircraft frames (much stronger and lighter than aluminum or steel) from soft coal.

Capturing even a fraction of that potential in our personal, team or business transformation efforts would provide a great ROI. But while these natural systems have the built-in DNA for transformation, humans have free will, so we must understand and apply these principles appropriately to achieve similar results. Just as natural transformations reflect different dynamics in each phase of change, an understanding of each organizational phase and the unique dynamics required for growth in each are critical to effective leadership. And a leader's moral character and courage are especially central during times of uncertainty and volatility, as they serve as a firm foundation to mitigate the fear and anxiety humans experience during change.

I've named the major transitions between life cycle phases metapoints, as "meta" was the stone post marking the turns at either end of the spina in ancient Roman chariot races. These turning points around gilded columns were where spectacular crashes were common, often ending in the death

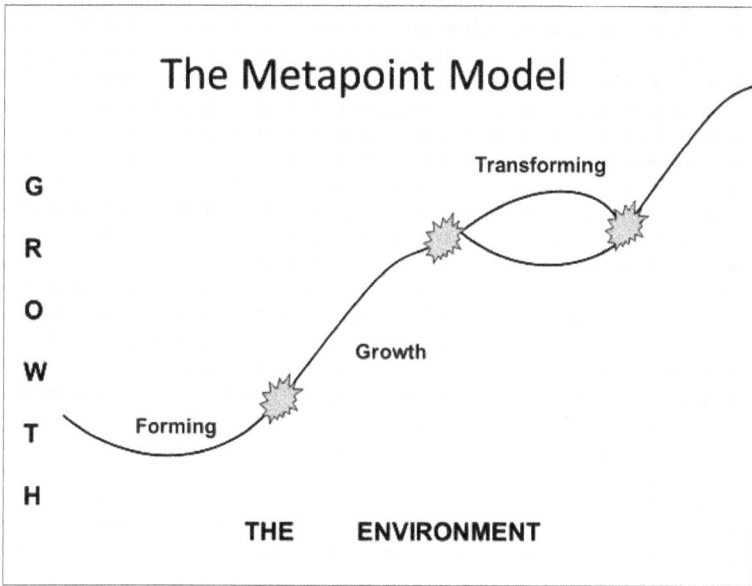

The Metapoint Model

G

R

O

W

T

H

Transforming

Growth

Forming

THE ENVIRONMENT

or serious injury of the drivers. In organizational life cycles as well, these turning points present both the greatest danger and opportunity, as they require significant shifts in leadership and management approaches to continue the growth of the organization and capture its potential. In essence the forming and transformation phases should be focused on effectiveness (exploring the environment and rapidly adapting to discover the right things that will produce the highest ROI from the environment), while the growth phase should be focused on efficiency (creating structures and processes to focus the organization on applying what has been learned to maximize growth while the environment is responding favorably).

As a disruptive entrepreneur Steve Jobs excelled in the forming phase (where rapid learning, rather than success, should be the main objective) but was so ineffective in leading a transition into the growth phase (creating structure and processes to apply that learning) that he lost the top job at the very company he founded. To his credit he learned well during his hiatus and returned to lead Apple successfully through a transformation phase. John Scully, who became CEO when Jobs was ousted by the board at Apple, came from a company (PepsiCo) in a long and stable growth phase and scaled Apple from 800 million USD in sales to 8 billion until he also encountered a metapoint beyond his leadership style and skills.

If we wish to replicate the transformational potential of natural systems, the ability to recognize leading indicators to an approaching metapoint is a key to navigating them effectively. Winning chariot drivers, as in horse racing today, had the ability to survey the field and position themselves appropriately before these dangerous meta turns. Those who were reactive and tried to correct in the middle of the turn were doomed to lose, crash and perhaps even die.

The most challenging of these metapoints for most leaders is the one requiring transformation. In no small part because it is easy to become so enamored with success in the growth phase that we miss the leading indicators of diminishing returns from the very leadership and management approaches that led to our success. Many leaders recognize these signs too late to avoid disastrous crashes, but the leading indicators of the need for transformation are there if you:

- *Recognize that all data (to include financial, customer and HR) is historical and that you cannot be ahead of the transformation curve if you are driving while looking primarily in your rearview mirror.* The predictive value of data diminishes as the environment begins to shift more rapidly near the end of a growth phase. What was an appropriate priority and valuable tool for scaling effectively during a growth phase can cause you to crash and burn if not perceived and treated differently as the need for transformation approaches.

- *Understand that almost all leading indicators of the need for transformation will be qualitative, human and intuitive.* They will be present for the discerning leader long before they are reflected in engagement surveys, customer satisfaction numbers or financial ledgers. They will appear in "insignificant" conversations with employees or customers, increased internal political maneuvering, competition for diminishing resources, increases in internal blaming and scapegoating, etc. Most leaders miss these early warning signs because their primary focus is on the lagging quantifiable indicators.

As previously referenced, it was Lincoln's focus on these human leading indicators, and his priority of touching and learning from the human environment on the frontlines so frequently, that enabled him to be such an adaptive, agile and effective leader during a transformational challenge to rival any in history. Absent this leadership style it is highly unlikely that he would have come to appreciate the value of enlisting black soldiers (which he developed directly from frontline accounts of their role in the South), nor would the vast majority of soldiers have embraced his vision of fighting not just to preserve the Union, but for freedom. In fact, you can correlate the percentage of time Lincoln spent away from the White House and in the field with the major challenges and turning points during the war,[145] indicative once again of his deep understanding of both human nature and adaptive leadership.

And of course, the further ahead of an approaching metapoint your leadership vision and intervention, the less chaotic and traumatic this process will be for the organization. That proactive vision cannot exist, however, absent the moral clarity to see and understand the human dynamics that predict the need for more than incremental change, or absent the intuitive decision-making ability and courage that is developed only through years of moral learning and growth. Those who lack such vision, moral clarity and courage will be late in recognizing a metapoint and likely to propose the typical leadership "solutions" to the diminishing performance that appears as a growth phase ends. Those include:

- Blaming individuals for systemic issues.
- Rewarding command and control leaders able to wring the last drops of blood (performance) out of people in a dying model.
- Reducing strategic investments, especially in training and development, just when people most need new skills.

- Leading a retreat to "what made us successful in the first place" as if the environment will ever shift back in time to its former conditions.

In stark contrast to these typical leadership approaches there is a "beyond the complexity" path to successful transformation that mirrors the leadership of Lincoln and avoids the well documented 70% plus failure rate in change efforts. This path to success requires:

- Formal leaders that have a concrete and compelling leadership vision that pulls (rather than tries to push) people through this more chaotic and intimidating phase of change. This requires a leadership vision of how success and contribution will be deepened by the change, not just disrupted. More importantly, it requires a vision that touches and engages the deeply embedded universal values in the human heart, which means that it requires a leader with the exceptional moral awareness and clarity to develop such a vision.

- Utilizing informal leaders close to the operating environment, as their frontline knowledge is invaluable to help a leader identify what the organization should leave behind, preserve and strengthen, and reach out for. They are also valuable in convincing skeptics to embrace the somewhat chaotic process of rapid decisions and constructive conflict required for the quick learning and adaptation necessary to transform rather than die.

- That you focus on supporting the small wins required to build critical mass, rather than more on trying to eliminate resistance to change. Too much attention and effort focused on resistance just feeds the negative fractals (energy) and increases the potential for a slow death. Invest in getting the positive DNA foundation right and trust the natural process, let the old caterpillar fade away from neglect and starvation. Lincoln could have spent all of his time and energy fighting the resistance to his ideas, instead he had an uncanny understanding of human nature and change and thus capitalized on opportunities to advance his ideas wherever and with whomever possible.

- That you don't try to change the entire organization in one major effort, as an abundance of evidence indicates the significant costs, both monetary and human, as well as the futility of this approach. A smaller initial scale allows for agility and adaptation at the speed of learning, which is critical to success. It also allows for a speed and scale that people can absorb while giving them the time and space to process effectively the emotional grief cycle that inevitably accompanies change. You can't rush or shortcut the natural laws of human nature without dire consequences.

Lincoln's deep appreciation for the importance of this point was evident in his timing of the Emancipation Proclamation, about which he stated: "It is my conviction that, had the proclamation been issued even six months earlier than it was, public sentiment would not have sustained it." He expressed similar thoughts about the timing of enlisting black troops in the border states, saying that should one "attempt to force the process, and he may spoil both fruit and tree."[146]

The successful transformation effort at Aetna in the early 2000's, often characterized as the most dramatic and successful in U.S. business, illustrates the value and validity of these principles.[147] The new CEO John Rowe never even announced a change effort, understanding that employees would interpret such an announcement as "we need to change," and naturally resist that message. He simply trusted these natural laws and principles to work, understanding that you do not reap the harvest immediately after sowing the seeds. Thus, change and transformation need not be complicated to understand or execute if we follow natural laws and the wisdom to be gleaned from thousands of years of human nature, while refusing to compromise moral clarity or courage as many do under the pressures of change. The right "small" moves, at the right time in the life cycle, can produce the leverage, critical mass and results needed for your organization to reach its full potential.

On A Personal Note

There are three questions that can help us use chaos and crisis, whether personal, business or global, as a refining fire to accelerate our growth and reach our higher potential.

What Should I Leave Behind?

We all accumulate baggage, clutter and waste in our lives and businesses over time. When things are laid bare is the best time to see clearly what no longer, and perhaps never, added real value to our personal and professional lives...and leave it in the ashes where it belongs. Inside the chrysalis, where one of nature's more striking transformations occurs, the cater-pillar almost completely disappears, leaving behind only a few cells that contain the DNA required to create a new butterfly. "Leaving behind" is the first and foundational step required for transformation, yet for humans and organizations also the most difficult. Wisdom is knowing when our scenario or the environment changes so much that we cannot move forward with the same attitudes, behaviors, strategies, processes...or sometimes even people...that we have held onto for so long without sacrificing our moral integrity and our growth potential.

As previously discussed, Nelson Mandela used his imprison-ment to leave behind the limiting beliefs and behavior of his earlier years to emerge from prison with little resemblance to the man who had entered twenty-seven years earlier. Rather than justify and compound his resentment and bitterness over oppression and injustice, the typical reaction to such harsh imprisonment and forced labor, he transformed himself from a man who formerly led a violent opposition to a leader who exemplified peace and forgiveness by letting go of unproduc-tive beliefs and behaviors. This transformation enabled him not only to become a trusted and respected leader to fellow prisoners, guards and wardens, but to bring together former adversaries and enemies to forge a new unified government in South Africa that transformed an entire nation.

What Should I Take With Me?

It is easy in the midst of chaos and uncertainty to act out of desperation, as our emotions tend to vacillate and our rational dimension shifts into overdrive trying to calculate odds and responses. But it is critical to guard against acting out of such desperation that we pursue paths that do not reflect our higher purpose, that compromise our moral integrity, or that fail to capitalize on our unique gifts. Important because those paths have no deep roots and thus cannot produce the enduring beauty and impact that we seek.

The flowers and grasses photographed by Lowe sprung quickly from the ashes because their seeds were protected and thus able to survive what appeared to be certain death. Crisis and chaos are great times to reflect on the seeds we have planted in years gone by with our values, because the full implications of our past values and priorities are more clearly revealed in such times. We must then identify and protect at all costs the values and priorities that strengthen our moral integrity as we explore new paths, and just as importantly, carefully prioritize the relative importance of those values. Only then can new and enduring beauty spring from the ashes more quickly than we anticipate, and also have the strength to endure.

What Should I Reach Out For?

When nature clears out the underbrush it creates the opportunity for new growth to flourish. In chaos or crisis there is the opportunity to explore and pursue new relationships and alliances to help us emerge stronger and accelerate our growth. But we can't see those possibilities if our head is down. We must have the faith, hope and courage to explore the new environment and continue adapting to the feedback it provides until we find the right synergy between the new conditions and our core capabilities and purpose.

This requires embracing conflict, risk, failure, collaboration and rapid decision-making, all with the goal of accelerated learning and adaptation rather than immediate success. This is counter intuitive, as most people seek greater certainty and security during times of chaos and challenge. Courageous and effective leaders, however, do not fall for the illusion of certainty, they blaze a trail forward to ground that is truly higher, safer and more sustainable, both for themselves and others. They are able to go forward, rather than retreat or bury their hand in the sand, in both personal and organizational crucibles because they are viewing the scenario with the longer and richer perspective that comes from their journey to the moral high ground. Leaders understand that freshly burned ground holds opportunities today that may soon disappear.

Many of nature's "miraculous" transformations occur at the point where chaos, heat and disruptive pressures appear to be in full control with no chance for survival, much less a positive outcome. If we look beyond appearances, however, at the atomic level it's not so dramatic. Graphite and diamonds, for example, despite their vast differences in properties and value, are both constituted of carbon atoms. That carbon structure remains after the transformation except for a "small" change in the bonding configuration that integrates and aligns the atoms. But it was the right change, at the right time, under great duress, to produce an extraordinary leap in strength, beauty and value. I can think of no better illustration of the power of transforming an unhealthy soular system into one that is aligned and integrated as intended.

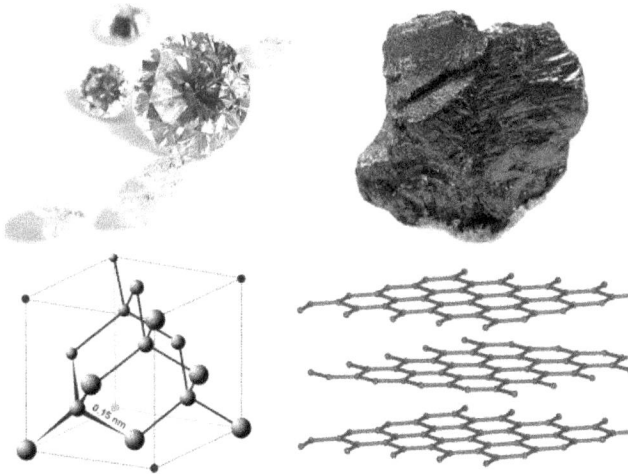

But to replicate these amazing transformations that occur in nature we must explore any changing or new environment with optimism and faith, no matter how foreign or daunting it may appear, and then act decisively to answer what we should leave behind, take with us and reach out for. Optimism and faith because nature teaches us that miraculous transformations in the midst of chaos and crisis are not only possible, but not as difficult or daunting as they appear. But such transformations do require moral clarity, courage and decisive leadership that often runs counter to human nature as well as to popular thought and culture.

And they require a perspective on challenge, chaos, crisis and suffering that is positive and hopeful in spite of the moment. This perspective is born of the deep understanding that meaning, fulfillment, character formation, and even happiness flourish when we face our crucibles with the proper psychological perspective and moral actions.[148] The suffering and defeats of Lincoln, including the death of his son and the depths of his depression, along with the challenges and pain encountered by Mandela, Martin Luther King Jr. and other great leaders need no recounting here, as with them I'm sure you are quite familiar. William Herndon, Lincoln's legal partner, said that to Lincoln the suffering from his depression was "medicinal and educational." A lifetime of dealing with this affliction built in him the patience, strength, resilience and depth of insight required to produce the unconventional decisions that saved a nation. His story, and those of other great leaders, validate the incredible strength and growth that comes from navigating the storms of life with moral clarity and courage.

Some of us have survived such storms and some of us have been broken. But a rainbow only appears after light has been broken (refracted) by passing through water droplets after a storm, yet the light is not diminished, but transformed into a richer and brighter beauty. The glorious lights in our lives, our relationships and gifts, are meant to shine even brighter after we are broken. Our appreciation for them richer and our understanding of their value and beauty deeper. But to see a rainbow a very precise angle of vision is required. What is your perspective on life's challenges and crucibles?

Joseph Campbell shares an instructive perspective in *A Joseph Campbell Companion: Reflections on the Art of Living* when he says:

"Nietzsche was the one who did the job for me. At a certain moment in his life, the idea came to him of what he called 'the love of your fate.' Whatever your fate is, whatever the hell happens, you say, "This is what I need." It may look like a wreck, but go at it as though it were an opportunity, a challenge. If you bring love to that moment – not discouragement – you will find the strength is there. Any disaster you can survive is an improvement in your character, your stature, and your life. What a privilege! This is when the spontaneity of your own nature will have a chance to flow. Then, when looking back at your life, you will see that the moments which seemed to be great failures followed by wreckage were the incidents that shaped the life you have now. You'll see that this is really true. Nothing can happen to you that is not positive. Even though it looks and feels at the moment like a negative crisis, it is not. The crisis throws you back, and when you are required to exhibit strength, it comes. The dark night of the soul comes just before revelation. When everything is lost, and all seems darkness, then comes the new life and all that is needed."

I would encourage you to read the Harvard Business School Working Knowledge article entitled "What the Stockdale Paradox Tells Us About Crisis Leadership,"[149] which highlights some of the lessons that enabled Admiral James Stockdale to not only survive seven and a half years as a POW in Vietnam, but to make that horrific period of suffering a defining step forward in his life. When interviewed by Jim Collins about how such suffering could be so transformative he said, *"I never lost faith in the end of the story. I never doubted not only that I would get out, but also that I would prevail in the end and turn the experience into the defining event of my life, which, in retrospect, I would not trade."* There is a lot to be learned from a leader who would not go back and trade over seven years of his life as a prisoner of war for something most of us would view as infinitely better. Stockdale had the wisdom to understand and apply the lessons of human history rather than to view himself as some unique victim of circumstance entitled to make exceptions to universal moral values and natural laws.

"You must never confuse faith that you will prevail in the end, which you can never afford to lose, with

> *the discipline to confront the most brutal facts of*
> *your current reality, whatever they might be."*
> — **Admiral James Stockdale**

Admiral Stockdale further elaborated on this perspective when he stated that:

"A properly educated leader, especially when harassed and under pressure, will know from his study of history and the classics that circumstances very much like those he is encountering have occurred from time to time on this earth since the beginning of history. He will avoid the self-indulgent error of seeing himself in a predicament so unprecedented, so unique, as to justify his making an exception to law, custom or morality in favor of himself. The making of such exceptions has been the theme of public life throughout much of our lifetimes. For twenty years, we've been surrounded by gamesmen unable to cope with the wisdom of the ages. They make exceptions to law and custom in favor of themselves because they choose to view ordinary dilemmas as unprecedented crises."

When I was a young lad my brother and I would go fishing on Lake Pee Wee (a big lake) in the small town where we lived. I was eager to escape a difficult home life, so I would sit on the shore and imagine that I could sail into the morning fog and reach any distant port I dreamed. I was so young, however, that I was afraid to venture out onto the water, as I feared the fog so thick that we could not navigate safely. I was viewing an ordinary human dilemma as an unprecedented crisis. Thankfully, an older friend was along, and as soon as we got out on the water we were able to navigate just fine, as the fog was much thicker in appearance than in reality.

We often sit on the shore and fear to venture into what appears to be a thick and dangerous fog. "Tell the people to go forward!" That was the response of God to Moses when the Israelites cried out for divine help as they stood legs locked and feet trembling on the shore of the Red Sea. The path becomes clear, and divine assistance available, only after we go forward into the fog by faith.

Nothing is more important than to remember, no matter the suffering or pressures of the moment, that natural laws of transformation and universal moral values put the wisdom of the ages at your disposal. And to have full faith that following this wisdom will produce enduring and transformational beauty and influence. My purpose and hope in writing this book is that you will respect and honor this timeless wisdom so that, eventually, when you reap what you have sown, it will be a happy and bountiful harvest.

Reflection & Action

The following exercise has helped many participants in our leadership programs to better answer the questions of what should I leave behind, take with me and reach out for.

Future Shock: Having identified your primary gaps in moral clarity and courage, write in plain language the implications of not addressing those gaps over the rest of your life. In other words, what will your life look like years from now if those gaps are not closed? Include the personal and professional implications for both yourself, your family and key relationships, and for those you lead.

Field of Dreams: Now write how your life will change for the better, in all the areas addressed above, when you begin to close those moral gaps and grow in your influence, emotional intelligence and inner peace.

You will find it useful to keep these documents handy and refer to them periodically, as we are all motivated by pain and pleasure. Thus the more clearly you describe the future implications in both these documents, and update them as needed, the more compelling they will be.

Finale
No Country for Old Men

At the beginning of No Country for Old Men, Sheriff Bell (Tommy Lee Jones) talks about how much he enjoyed hearing about the old-timers in law enforcement, some with such moral courage and influence that they did not even carry a gun. But by the end of the movie Bell feels overmatched in a culture where moral clarity is lacking and people do what feels good in the moment, no matter who suffers.

In the movie's final scene he shares a dream about his father, now long passed away, who rides past him on horseback in the mountains, carrying a flame out into the cold and darkness of the night. But despite the lack of a single word from his father, Bell knew that he was going ahead to make a fire for them, saying, "I knew that when I got there, he'd be there."

If you watch the movie or this final scene on YouTube, tell me, have you ever heard a statement spoken with more certainty?

The flame his father carried represented the moral values that Sheriff Bell had learned from the old-timers. Values that ensured a strong measure of trust and respect from others and that produced a sense of security and certainty in a better future.

Now, however, surveys indicate increasing cynicism, and even despair, in our culture. Too many are wandering aimlessly, lost amidst the cold and darkness of moral ambivalence and uncertainty. We desperately need leaders that will carry the light, warmth and power of moral clarity and courage ahead to show the way. Leaders who are not blown about with the winds of change or popular culture. Leaders with a bright and unwavering flame.

Given that on average we interact with over a thousand people during our lifetime, we are only two nodes away from touching the lives of a million people. We can never know how many lost souls will see our singular bright flame and follow that shining light to safety and higher ground.

Godspeed on your journey.

Roy Holley
August 2022
Moralleadership.us

Selected Bibliography for Abraham Lincoln

Basler Roy P., ed. 1953. *The Collected Works of Abraham Lincoln.* 8 vols. New Brunswick, N.J.: Rutgers University Press.

Guelzo, Allen C. 2003. *Abraham Lincoln : Redeemer President.* Grand Rapids, Mich.: Eerdmans.

Kearns, Doris. 2013. *Team of Rivals : The Political Genius of Abraham Lincoln.* London: Penguin.

White, Ronald C. 2009. *A. Lincoln.* New York: Random House.

Miller, William L. 2002. *Lincoln's Virtues : An Ethical Biography.* New York: Knopf.

Note: These are the most exhaustive and relevant works on Lincoln I found for the purposes of this book. Many other helpful sources are included in the endnotes. The Collected Works of Abraham Lincoln (8 vols.) may be found online at https://quod.lib.umich.edu/l/lincoln/. Over 40,000 Lincoln documents and links to expert resources may be found online in The Library of Congress at https://www.loc.gov/collections/abraham-lincoln-papers/.

Endnotes

1   Lennick, Doug, and Fred Kiel Ph.D. 2011. *Moral Intelligence 2.0.* Pearson Prentice Hall. (see pages 35-37).
2   Schwartz, Shalom. 2012. "An Overview of the Schwartz Theory of Basic Values." *Online Readings in Psychology and Culture,* 2 (1).
3   Kinnier, Richard T., Jerry L. Kernes, and Therese M. Dautheribes. 2000. "A Short List of Universal Moral Values." *Counseling and Values* 45 (1): 4–16.
4   Johnson, Robert, and Adam Cureton. 2004. "Kant's Moral Philosophy." Stanford Encyclopedia of Philosophy. February 23, 2004.
5   Burlingame, Michael. 2013. *Abraham Lincoln : A Life.* Baltimore, Maryland: The Johns Hopkins University Press. Volume 2, p. 9.
6   Museum, Abraham Lincoln Presidential. "Lincoln Note Offers Glimpse into His Idea of Democracy."
7   "Latest National Business Ethics Survey Reveals Looming Ethics Downturn in Corporate America." www.halklailiskiler. com.
8   "GBES 2023." Ethics & Compliance Initiative, www.ethics. org/gbes-2023/.
9   Edelman. 2023. "2023 Edelman Trust Barometer."

10 "The State of Moral Leadership in Business 2018 HOW Metrics®: New Metrics for a New Reality -Rethinking the Source of Resiliency, Innovation, and Growth." https://tinyurl.com/3v5h5sh8.

11 Bailey, Catherine. 2016. "What Makes Work Meaningful — or Meaningless." MIT Sloan Management Review.

12 Jensen, Keld. 2013. "Three Shocking Truths about Lying at Work." Forbes.

13 Ekman, Paul. 2009. *Telling Lies : Clues to Deceit in the Marketplace, Politics, and Marriage*. New York, Ny: W.W. Norton.

14 Ariely, Dan. 2013. *The (Honest) Truth about Dishonesty : How We Lie to Everyone--Especially Ourselves*. New York: Harper Perennial.

15 Taylor, Charles. 2018. *A Secular Age*. Cambridge ; London: The Belknap Press Of Harvard University Press.

16 Tiku, Nitasha. 2019. "Three Years of Misery inside Google, the Happiest Company in Tech." Wired.

17 Burlingame, Michael. 2013. *Abraham Lincoln : A Life*. Vol. 2, p. 718. Baltimore, Maryland: The Johns Hopkins University Press.

18 Bigelow, John. 1909. *Retrospections of an Active Life,* p. 367.

19 Winger, Stewart, ed. 2001. Review of *Lincoln's Economics and the American Dream: A Reappraisal. Journal of the Abraham Lincoln Association,* 22 (1): 50–80.

20 Wilson, Douglas L, Rodney O Davis, Terry Wilson, eds. 1998. *Herndon's Informants : Letters, Interviews, and Statements about Abraham Lincoln*. Urbana: University Of Illinois Press. p. 238.

21 Douglass, Frederick, and Henry Louis Gates. 1994. *Frederick Douglas: Autobiographies*. New York: Literacy Classics Of The United States, p. 785.

22 Miller, William L. 2003. *Lincoln's Virtues : An Ethical Biography*, pp. 40-41. New York: Vintage Books.

23 "Abraham Lincoln's Values and Philosophy –
    Abraham Lincoln's Classroom." http://www.
    abrahamlincolnsclassroom.org/abraham-lincoln-in-depth/
    abraham-lincolns-values-and-philosophy/.

24 Beveridge, Albert. 1928. *Abraham Lincoln*. Vol. 1, p. 540.
    Houghton Mifflin.

25 Basler, Roy. 1990. *The Collected Works of Abraham Lincoln,
    1:282*. New Brunswick: Rutgers University Press.

26 "Emancipation Proclaimed." October 1862. *Douglas Monthly*.
    https://rbscp.lib.rochester.edu/4406

27 Miller, William L. 2003. *Lincoln's Virtues : An Ethical
    Biography*, p. 397. New York: Vintage Books.

28 Fleener, John. 1997. Review of *The Relationship between
    the MBTI and Measures of Personality and Performance in
    Management Groups*. In *Developing Leaders: Research and
    Applications in Psychological Type and Leadership Development*,
    edited by C. Fitzgerald and A. Kirby, 115–38. Davies-Black.

29 "The Naturally Rational Brain? How People Use, and Lose,
    Preexisting Biases to Make Decisions." Zuckermaninstitute.
    columbia.edu. 2018.

30 Miller, William L. 2003. *Lincoln's Virtues : An Ethical
    Biography*, p. 400. New York: Vintage Books.

31 "Joshua Greene." https://www.joshua-greene.net/.

32 "Resources." NARM Training Institute. https://narmtraining.
    com/resources/.

33 Lench, H. C., Reed, N. T., George, T., Kaiser, K. A., &
    North, S. G. (2023). "Anger has benefits for attaining
    goals." *Journal of personality and social psychology*, 10.1037/
    pspa0000350. Advance online publication.

34 "Lincoln's Unsent Letter to George Meade." 2014. American
    Battlefield Trust. https://www.battlefields.org/learn/
    primary-sources/lincolns-unsent-letter-george-meade.

35 LeDoux, Joseph E. and Richard Brown. 2017. "A Higher-Order Theory of Emotional Consciousness." *Proceedings of the National Academy of Sciences* 114 (10): E2016–25.

36 Bajaj, Sahil, and William D.S. Killgore. 2021. "Association between Emotional Intelligence and Effective Brain Connectome: A Large-Scale Spectral DCM Study." *NeuroImage* 229 (April): 117750.

37 "Emotional Intelligence, Emotional Hijacks, and Systems Thinking." www.linkedin.com. https://www.linkedin.com/pulse/emotional-intelligence-hijacks-systems-thinking-daniel-goleman/.

38 "Moral Cognition." Joshua Greene. https://www.joshua-greene.net/research/moral-cognition/.

39 "Faculty Profile > USC Dana and David Dornsife College of Letters, Arts and Sciences." 2014. Usc.edu. 2014. https://dornsife.usc.edu/cf/faculty-and-staff/faculty.cfm?pid=1008328.

40 News, M. I. T. 2019. "MRI Sensor Images Deep Brain Activity." MIT McGovern Institute.

41 Resnick, Brian. 2016. "There's a Lot of Junk FMRI Research out There. Here's What Top Neuroscientists Want You to Know." Vox.

42 News, M. I. T. 2019. "MRI Sensor Images Deep Brain Activity." MIT McGovern Institute.

43 "Mirror Neurons: The Most Hyped Concept in Neuroscience? | Psychology Today." 2012. www.psychologytoday.com.

44 Passingham, Richard. 2009. "How Good Is the Macaque Monkey Model of the Human Brain?" *Current Opinion in Neurobiology* 19 (1): 6–11.

45 "Neuro-Fiction: A Guide to Dissecting Overblown Neuroscience Headlines | TED Blog." https://blog.ted.com/spotting-neuro-fiction-a-guide-to-dissecting-overblown-neuroscience-headlines/.

46   Gilbert, Roberta, Sally Satel, and Scott Lilienfeld. 2015. "From the Director's Corner through the Lens #15 -Winter 2015 Brain Science-What It Can and Cannot Deliver. Brainwashed, the Seductive Appeal of Mindless Neuroscience." http://www.hsystems.org/resources/ Through+the+Lens+15_Winter+2015.pdf

47   Garrett, Neil, Stephanie C Lazzaro, Dan Ariely, and Tali Sharot. 2016. "The Brain Adapts to Dishonesty." *Nature Neuroscience* 19 (12): 1727–32.

48   Nichols, Thomas E., and Jean-Baptist Poline. 2009. "Puzzlingly High Correlations in FMRI Studies of Emotion, Personality, and Social Cognition." *Perspectives on Psychological Science* 4 (3): 291–93.

49   "New Research Determines Who You Can Trust the Most | Psychology Today." www.psychologytoday.com.

50   Christensen, Clayton. 2019. "How Will You Measure Your Life?" Harvard Business Review.

51   Bender, Crhistian Luis, Xingxing Sun, Muhammad Farooq, Qian Yang, Caroline Davison, Matthieu Maroteaux, Yi-shuian Huang, Yoshihiro Ishikawa, and Siqiong June Liu. 2020. "Emotional Stress Induces Structural Plasticity in Bergmann Glial Cells via an AC5–CPEB3–GluA1 Pathway." *Journal of Neuroscience* 40 (17): 3374–84.

52   "Even in the Healthy, Stress Causes Brain to Shrink, Yale Study Shows." medicine.yale.edu.

53   "Stress Eats Holes in Your Brain." 2018. https:// centerforbrainhealth.org/article/stress-eats-holes-in-your-brain.

54   "Pay, Power and Politics: Where Did Carlos Ghosn Go Wrong?" Knowledge@Wharton. https://knowledge.wharton. upenn.edu/article/carlos-ghosn-out-at-nissan/.

55   McLain, Sean. 2018. "Nissan Probe Alleges Ghosn Used Company Money to Buy Homes, Enrich His Sister." Wall Street Journal.

56   Solzhenitsȳn, Aleksandr Isaevich, Thomas P Whitney, H T
     Willetts, Edward E Ericson, and Jordan B Peterson. 2018. *The
     Gulag Archipelago 1918-56 : An Experiment in Literary
     Investigation.* London: Vintage Classics.

57   *The New York Times.* 2018. "Opinion | the Writer Who
     Destroyed an Empire."

58   Senge, Peter M. 1994. *The Fifth Discipline Fieldbook :
     Strategies and Tools for Building a Learning Organization.* New
     York: Currency, Doubleday.

59   Washington, D. 1975. "NATIONAL TRANSPORTATION
     SAFETY BOARD MARINE ACCIDENT REPORT SS
     EDMUND FITZGERALD SINKING in LAKE SUPERIOR
     UNITED STATES GOVERNMENT Title and Subtitle:
     Marine Accident Report SS EDMUND FITZGERALD
     Sinking in Lake Superior On." https://www.michiganseagrant.
     org/downloads/lessons/datasets/earthscience/Edmund-
     Fitzgerald-accident-report-NTSBR.pdf.

60   Rushe, Dominic. 2020. "Boeing's 'Culture of Concealment'
     Led to Fatal 737 Max Crashes, Report Finds." *The Guardian*,
     March 6, 2020, sec. Business.

61   "So Your Company Has a Vision: Why Can't Everyone See
     It?" Knowledge at Wharton. https://knowledge.wharton.
     upenn.edu/article/company-vision-cant-everyone-see/.

62   "Abraham Lincoln's Temperance Address of 1842." www.
     abrahamlincolnonline.org. https://www.abrahamlincolnonline.
     org/lincoln/speeches/temperance.htm.

63   Eavis, Peter. 2020. "As the Pandemic Forced Layoffs, C.E.O.s
     Gave up Little." *The New York Times*, July 29, 2020, sec.
     Business.

64   "Employee Loyalty Is Strongly Tied to How Employers
     Handled COVID-19, New Guardian Life Research Finds |
     Guardian." 2021. Guardianlife.com. 2021.

65   Steare, Roger, Pavlos Stamboulides, Peter Lewis, Lysbeth Plas,
     Petra Wilton, and Patrick Woodman. 2014. "THE MORAL

DNA of PERFORMANCE." https://www.managers.org.
uk/wp-content/uploads/2014/10/The-MoralDNA-of-
Performance-October-2014.pdf.

66 Schein, Edgar H. 2017. *Organizational Culture and
Leadership*. 5th ed. Hoboken, New Jersey: Wiley.

67 Griffith, Erin. 2020. "Airbnb Was like a Family, until the
Layoffs Started." *The New York Times*, July 17, 2020, sec.
Technology.

68 Zak, Paul J. 2017. "The Neuroscience of Trust." Harvard
Business Review.

69 "'It's Churchillian': Lessons from Ukraine's Military
Commander-In-Chief." 2022. StrategicCHRO360.com

70 "Culture Fit Is Outdated. It's Time to Think about Culture
Add." 2020. Washington Post.

71 Hofmans, Joeri, and Timothy A. Judge. 2019. "Hiring for
Culture Fit Doesn't Have to Undermine Diversity." Harvard
Business Review.

72 "What the Research Says about Cultural Alignment in
Hiring." Talent Management. https://www.talentmgt.com.

73 "Our Code of Conduct." FedEx.com.

74 "Hiring at Apple for Organizational Culture Fit." www.
interviewedge.com. https://www.interviewedge.com/articles/
Hiring-at-Apple-for-Culture-Fit.htm.

75 Schwantes, Marcel. 2018. "Warren Buffett Says Integrity Is
the Most Important Trait to Hire For. Ask These 12 Questions
to Find It." Inc.com.

76 "Training the Talented, the Ritz-Carlton Way." 2019. Amanet.
org.

77 "Simon Sinek: What Should Your Company Culture Be? Start
with Verbs." BigThink.com

78 "How Avoiding Shadow Values Can Help Change Your
Organisational Culture." www.aicd.com.au.

79 Wilkinson, David. 2017. "The Step-By-Step Guide to How
Unethical Behaviour Develops." The Oxford Review.

80   Knoll, Michael, Robert G. Lord, Lars-Eric Petersen, and Oliver Weigelt. 2015. "Examining the Moral Grey Zone: The Role of Moral Disengagement, Authenticity, and Situational Strength in Predicting Unethical Managerial Behavior." *Journal of Applied Social Psychology* 46 (1): 65–78.

81   Katzenbach, Jon, Ilona Steffen, and Caroline Kronley. 2014. "Cultural Change That Sticks." Harvard Business Review.

82   "Fraud and Deception Detection: Five Language Fingerprints." 2021. CFA Institute Enterprising Investor.

83   Sull, Donald, Charles Sull, William Cipolli, and Caio Brighenti. 2022. "Why Every Leader Needs to Worry about Toxic Culture." *MIT Sloan Management Review*.

84   "Great Frauds in History: Quentin Thomas Wiles and MiniScribe." 2019. MoneyWeek.

85   Kinni, Theodore. 2022. "When It Comes to Changing Culture, Think Small." Strategy+Business.

86   "Diversity & Inclusion." FedEx.com

87   "Your Chief Diversity Officer Is Likely Leaving." Kornferry.com.

88   Garland, Ted Evanoff, Desiree Stennett and Max. 2020. "How 3 Memphis Companies Are Making Diversity and Inclusion a Priority." The Commercial Appeal.

89   Leslie, Lisa M. 2019. "Diversity Initiative Effectiveness: A Typological Theory of Unintended Consequences." *Academy of Management Review* 44 (3).

90   Gharbi, Musa al-. 2020. *"Review of Research Shows Diversity Training Is Typically Ineffective."* RealClear Science.

91   Ricki, Slott. 2022. "How a 28-Year-Old Is Fighting against 'Divisive' Anti-Racism Training." New York Post.

92   "Enchantment with Chloe Valdary | a Bit of Optimism with Simon Sinek: Episode 38." youtube.com.

93   Kutsch, Laura. 2019. "Can We Rely on Our Intuition?" Scientific American.

94   "Jeff Bezos and the Role of Intuition in Decision Making." RealTime Performance.

95 Schoultz, Mike. 2018. "An Einstein Story Showing What a Humble Man He Was." Medium.com.

96 "The Path to Critical Thinking." 2005. HBS Working Knowledge.

97 "4 Intriguing Decisions from Martin Luther King | Psychology Today Canada." 2014.

98 "Instinct in a World of Analytics | Virgin." 2019. Virgin.com.

99 "Ambrose Burnside." 2018. HISTORY.com

100 "NPR Choice Page." 2019.

101 Carpenter, Francis. 1866. *Six Months at the White House with Abraham Lincoln*, p.22.

102 Tarbell, Ida M. 1900. *The Life of Abraham Lincoln*, Vol. 3, p. 115.

103 "The Untold Story of the Battle for Kyiv." 2022. Small Wars Journal.

104 Melchior, Jillian Kay. 2022. "Opinion | the West Leaves Ukraine Outgunned against Russia." Wall Street Journal.

105 Henry Raymond to Abraham Lincoln, August 22, 1864. Lincoln Papers, Library of Congress. https://hd.housedivided. dickinson.edu/node/42201

106 Basler, Roy. 1990. *The Collected Works of Abraham Lincoln, 7:507.* New Brunswick: Rutgers University Press.

107 Waytz, Adam. 2016. "The Limits of Empathy." Harvard Business Review.

108 Friedman, Edwin H, Margaret M Treadwell, and Edward W Beal. 2017. *A Failure of Nerve : Leadership in the Age of the Quick Fix.* New York: Church Publishing.

109 Hougaard, Rasmus, Jacqueline Carter, and Marissa Afton. 2021. "Connect with Empathy, but Lead with Compassion." Harvard Business Review.

110 Bechtoldt, Myriam N., and Vanessa K. Schneider. 2016. "Predicting Stress from the Ability to Eavesdrop on Feelings: Emotional Intelligence and Testosterone Jointly Predict Cortisol Reactivity." *Emotion* 16 (6): 815–25.

111 Joly, Hubert. 2022. "5 Principles of Purposeful Leadership." Harvard Business Review.

112 Leinwand, Sally Blount and Paul. 2022. "Five Ways to Harness the Power of Purpose." Strategy+Business.

113 "The Price of Being Political." Kornferry.com.

114 George, Bill, Peter Sims, Andrew N. McLean, and Diana Mayer. 2007. "Discovering Your Authentic Leadership." Harvard Business Review.

115 Franklin, Benjamin. "The Autobiography of Benjamin Franklin." Sec. 9. Wikisource.

116 Welles, Gideon. 1911. *Diary of Gideon Welles*, Vol. 1, pp. 23-25.

117 Basler, Roy. 1990. *The Collected Works of Abraham Lincoln, 5:388-389*. New Brunswick: Rutgers University Press.

118 Doris Kearns Goodwin. 2018. *Leadership in Turbulent Times, p. 225*. New York: Simon & Schuster.

119 Basler, Roy. 1990. *The Collected Works of Abraham Lincoln, 2:81*. New Brunswick: Rutgers University Press.

120 Doris Kearns Goodwin. 2018. *Leadership in Turbulent Times, p. 106*. New York: Simon & Schuster.

121 Drucker, Peter F. 2005. "Managing Oneself." Harvard Business Review.

122 "Learning Humility from Lincoln | Psychology Today." 2012.

123 Baumeister, Roy F., Jennifer D. Campbell, Joachim I. Krueger, and Kathleen D. Vohs. 2003. "Does High Self-Esteem Cause Better Performance, Interpersonal Success, Happiness, or Healthier Lifestyles?" *Psychological Science in the Public Interest* 4 (1): 1–44.

124 "Imposter Syndrome's Unexpected Benefits." Wharton IDEAS Lab.

125 Owens, Bradley P., Angela S. Wallace, and David A. Waldman. 2015. "Leader Narcissism and Follower Outcomes: The Counterbalancing Effect of Leader Humility." *Journal of Applied Psychology* 100 (4): 1203–13.

126 Harvard Health Publishing. 2021. "Giving Thanks Can Make You Happier." Harvard Health.

127 Bariso, Justin. Review of *After a Historic Game, Patrick Mahomes Desperately Wanted to Speak with One Person. It's a Lesson in Emotional Intelligence.* Inc.com.

128 "'I'm Glorifying Him': Grounded by Faith, Mahomes Prays before Super Bowl Departure." 2020. WKRG News 5.

129 Sousa, Milton, and Dirk van Dierendonck. 2017. "Servant Leadership and the Effect of the Interaction between Humility, Action, and Hierarchical Power on Follower Engagement." *Journal of Business Ethics* 141 (1): 13–25.

130 White, Ronald C. 2009. *A. Lincoln : A Biography*, pp. 212-214. New York: Random House.

131 Wilson, Douglas L and Davis, Rodney O, eds. 1998. *Herndon's Informants : Letters, Interviews, and Statements about Abraham Lincoln, p. 166.* Urbana: University Of Illinois Press.

132 Hermann, Peter, Michael Smith, and Keith L. Alexander. 2015. "Horrified Passengers Witnessed Brutal July 4 Slaying Aboard Metro Car." *Washington Post*, July 7, 2015, sec. Local.

133 Ladyman, Ian. 2020. "Harry Gregg: Former Man United Goalkeeper's Final Interview." Mail Online. February 17, 2020.

134 "Margaret Thatcher and the Integrity of Leadership." 2005. Albertmohler.com.

135 Warrell, Dr Margie. 2013. "Margaret Thatcher: An Icon of Leadership Courage." Forbes.

136 "Margaret Thatcher – as Remarkable and Divisive in Death as She Was in Life." 2013. C. E. Lord OBE. April 8, 2013. https://edwardlord.org.

137 Thatcher, Margaret. 1995. "The Moral Foundations of Society." Imprimis. https://imprimis.hillsdale.edu/the-moral-foundations-of-society/.

138 "Baron Black of Crossharbour | Lord Conrad Black | the Jordan B. Peterson Podcast - S4: E:35." youtube.com.

139 Curzer, Howard. 1996. "The Open Repository @ Binghamton (the ORB) . The Society for Ancient Greek Philosophy Newsletter, Aristotle's Account of the Virtue of Courage in Nicomachean Ethics III.6-9." https://orb.binghamton.edu/cgi/viewcontent. cgi?article=1182&context=sagp.

140 "The Long Walk of Nelson Mandela - the Prisoner: Interview with Neville Alexander." FRONTLINE.

141 "The Long Walk of Nelson Mandela - the Prisoner: Interview with Strini Moodley (Excerpt)." FRONTLINE.

142 Usman, Zainab. 2013. "Mandela: The Personification of Humility, by Zainab Usman." Premium Times Nigeria.

143 "Mandela's Humility." Nieman Reports. https://niemanreports.org/articles/mandelas-humility/.

144 "These Heartening Photos Show the Bush Coming back to Life." 2020. NewsComAu. News.com.au.

145 Phillips, Donald T. 2009. *Lincoln on Leadership : Executive Strategies for Tough Times*, pp. 22-24. New York: Grand Central Publishing.

146 Carpenter, Francis. 1866. *Six Months at the White House with Abraham Lincoln*, p.77.

147 Katzenbach, Jon, Ilona Steffen, and Caroline Kronley. 2014. "Cultural Change That Sticks." Harvard Business Review.

148 Hall, M. Elizabeth Lewis, Richard Langer, and Jason Mcmartin. 2010. "The Role of Suffering in Human Flourishing: Contributions from Positive Psychology, Theology, and Philosophy." *Journal of Psychology and Theology* 38 (2): 111–21.

149 "What the Stockdale Paradox Tells Us about Crisis Leadership." 2020. HBS Working Knowledge.

Acknowledgements

Anyone who undertakes the writing of a book surely deepens their appreciation for all those who have influenced them and upon whose shoulders they stand. For me, relative to leadership, that appreciation begins with the opportunity to work for exceptional leaders like Fred Smith, Judith Rogala and Steve Friedrichs during my decade of leadership experience at FedEx. While a member of the FedEx Leadership Institute I was blessed to work with Steve Nielsen, Cesar Valenzuela, Michael Reed, et al. whose examples and ideas were instrumental in clarifying my life's mission and approach to leadership development.

Since leaving FedEx I have been profoundly blessed to work with the same team of gifted leaders and wonderful friends to deliver our signature leadership programs for over two decades. Indispensable to the success of these programs has been the enduring commitment and contributions of Rebecca Chou,

Judith Rogala, Michael O'Donnell, Hank Grimmick, Bill Catlette, Tammee Tuttle, Mike Gibbs and Steve Digges. It is impossible to express in mere words my appreciation for them.

While working in China I was fortunate to meet and collaborate in academic work with Dwight Hopkins and Marco Busi, both of whom have been generous in sharing their invaluable ideas and wisdom, along with their encouragement and support. Especially during the writing process the friendship and support of David Ross, Jeffrey McNulty and Harry Flaris has often kept me moving forward when challenges arose. Finally, my deepest appreciation to Bill Catlette for sharing his coaching and expertise as a successful author so generously with me from beginning to end of this process, and for his relentless faith in me, without which I may well have abandoned the effort.

And to Ghislain Viau of Creative Publishing Book Design, my gratitude for his expertise in the design and publishing phases for this book.

To God above I am most grateful for the blessing of so many wonderful people and exceptional leaders in my life.

Index